Contents

Previous double page:
A garden pool with an area for swimming. The wooden dock separates the swimming area in the back from the rest of the pool and serves as a diving board.

The World of Water

Preface

Important:
Please follow the suggestions presented in the Note of Warning on page 143 so that your enjoyment of your garden pool, stream, or water garden will be free of worry.

Do you feel drawn to water? If so, then you know how powerfully this element affects our senses. It stimulates at the same time that it calms us; we can hear it, smell it, taste it, and feel it on our skin. The hours spent near water count among our most enjoyable nature experiences. Whether we look out on the glittering sunlight and rippling surface of a lake, hear the rushing of a river, or listen to the murmur of a meadow brook, our everyday worries begin to recede, and we are filled instead with equanimity and peace, with happiness and joy.

You can enjoy this experience—on a small scale—in your own garden. This handbook shows you what you have to do. You will find that in addition to the traditional natural pond and formal garden pool a surprising number of variations are possible; to name a few: a pool incorporated into a terrace, a garden pool that doubles as a swimming pool, a play pool for the children, or a marsh bed in a mini-garden. If you want a very special experience, consider a brook running through your garden, wending its way in endless variations from its source to the pool. If you have enough space you can set up a water garden, complete with pools, water fountains, waterfalls, and marsh beds, all connected by a stream. Give your imagination free rein when you plan your pool; the required know-how for turning your dream into reality will be provided in this book.

A special feature of this illustrated handbook are its How-to pages, where everything to be done is both described step by step and shown in clear drawings, making the directions easy to follow even for nonexperts. In addition to learning how to build a pool, you will find out everything you need to know about the different ways the margins can be designed and constructed and about the most beautiful plants as well as the fish and other aquatic animals that can live in and around your garden pool. And last but not least, upkeep and wintering over of a pool and stream are discussed. This handbook not only offers competent advice and pleasant reading, but with its many color photos it is also a unique picture book of lovely pools for big and small gardens. The pictures show overall views and details and include the wide variety of plant and animal life found in and near pools.

In the photo:
Thriving vegetation along the edge of a garden pool. The blue flowers of pickerelweed peek out from the lush green of the leaves (in foreground). The spikes of purple loosestrife in the back form a striking color contrast.

Ponds in Nature and in Human Civilization

The Element Water

"The human soul resembles water; it descends from heaven, it rises to heaven, and has to descend to earth again, changing eternally back and forth." These lines are from the poem "Song of the Spirits above the Waters" by Johann Wolfgang von Goethe. Tranquility and wildness, sameness and change are qualities of water that fascinate us. We like to relax on the shore of a calm lake, we feel a pleasant shudder at the sight of water shooting down a gorge, we see in the flow of water a symbol of permanence as well as of change, renewal, and growth. Water can be a curse—if there is too much or too little of it—or a blessing that is beautifully expressed in a Turkmenian proverb that says "Throw a seed in your footstep, add a drop of water, and you will be rewarded with a rich harvest."

Without water there would be no life on Earth. Water not only covers 70 percent of the Earth's surface and, in the form of vapor, represents 4 percent of the atmosphere, but it also makes up 60 to 70 percent of the body substance of most organisms. The belief that water is the primal substance from which the world was created in the beginning is common to the religions of people everywhere. Along with this goes the belief that water is the source of life, health, and fertility.

The Sacredness of Water

For the people of ancient times water was something magical and venerable. In Greek and Roman mythology all bodies of water were thought to be inhabited by graceful, female nature spirits, or nymphs, which were worshiped at springs in glades and grottoes. The Celts regarded springs as well as streams, rivers, bogs, and lakes as sacred places. It was to these places that the Druids brought sacrificial gifts and where they offered up human sacrifices.

The Germanic sagas tell of fountains welling from under the three roots of the world tree Yggdrasil. From one of these fountains the Norns, Norse goddesses of fate, dipped holy, rejuvenating water with which they watered the world tree every morning so that it would retain its youthful, evergreen vitality and continue to bestow life-giving dew on the valleys.

No Civilizations Without Water

The first human cultures arose where there was water. Indeed, one could say that irrigation was the beginning of civilization. Thus the first high cultures evolved on the land between the Euphrates and the Tigris rivers from the cultivation of irrigated fields. This geographical area also boasted one of the seven wonders of the world, the Hanging Gardens of Babylon. They were said to have been a pleasure garden of exquisite luxury, consisting of elaborately built stone terraces adorned with a profusion of flowering plants and tropical trees and irrigated by a mechanical watering system. The Sumerians, the Babylonians, and the Assyrians achieved an amazing degree of sophistication in moving water mechanically.

The realm of the pharaohs, too, owed its power, fame, and wealth to water, the river Nile. "The oldest of the gods, the Nile, which created everything and which rises above its banks to give human beings life," an old Egyptian inscription reads. The palace gardens included water basins with lotus flowers floating in them.

Aqueducts still standing today in many places give us an inkling of the grandiose water delivery projects the Romans built throughout their empire. Water was an essential part of a Roman villa. It filled marble basins, was conducted through the garden in pipes, and made its appearance in the form of fountains and waterfalls.

China's emergence as a major civilization, too, began with irrigation or, more accurately, with the taming of the Yellow River or Hwang Ho. The high points of irrigation engineering coincided with the golden ages of Chinese culture. One material embodiment of that culture was the emperor's palace with its gardens, which were unparalleled in splendor, sumptuousness, and exquisite taste. Everything was artificially constructed but meant to appear as the work of nature: The course the water took imitated brooks and streams, and the lakes, complete with islands and protruding rocks, were made to look as natural as possible. The surface of the water mirroring back the sky was regarded as the heavens descending to Earth in visible form.

The Chinese gardens also influenced Japanese gardening. In Japan, a house and its garden have always been thought of as one harmonious, inseparable unit. This is immediately apparent in the basic structure of the houses: There are movable walls that open up so wide that inside and outside become one. Paths, ponds, brooks, bridges, and fences are set up to fit into the landscape naturally so that one ceases to be aware of them as human creations.

Morning mood near a pond. The grasses are still covered with frost, but the sun's rays are already warming them.

Water was also an important part of Arabian gardens. For a nomad, water was the greatest luxury life could offer. The owners of a garden pool could cup some water in their hands to cool their foreheads; they saw the sky mirrored in it; they listened to the music of the fountains. In the Alhambra, the palace of the Moorish kings in southern Spain, water, with its smooth, mirrorlike surface, adds light and space to the enclosed courtyards, and the lively bubbling of fountains in the gardens combine in a poetic and at the same time sensuous presence.

Baroque Gardens and English Parks

European gardens of the sixteenth and seventeenth centuries resembled the Roman gardens. They were planned by architects who chose to obey laws of design rather than follow the requirements of nature. Plants became part of the architectural scheme, that is, everything that grew beyond the predetermined shapes was trimmed away. Nor was water allowed to flow freely. It was contained in straight and rigid canals, hurled up into the air in sprays designed to attract admiring eyes, and guided down over stone steps in controlled cascades. In Baroque gardens, of which the most perfected examples were realized in France, everything depended on man's doing. If maintenance lapsed, these gardens quickly reverted to nature.

In England, the principle of Chinese gardening gained hold. The goal was to give everything as natural an appearance as possible, or to adapt the style of a formal garden to the surrounding landscape in such a way that the garden fit in harmoniously. The English parks or landscape gardens with their natural looking brooks and lakes became popular and were soon imitated everywhere.

An idyllic picture of late summer. What looks like nature's work here has been created by humans. A natural pond in the shape of a T forms the restful center of a garden that was established on an old field. The old trees were left standing. All that remains at this time of year of the profusely flowering yellow flag irises bordering the pool are the leaves.

Ponds and Pools in Nature

Like almost everything else that grows out of the human urge to imitate nature and create—and that is then proclaimed a human invention—garden ponds and pools have predecessors or models of various kinds in nature. Water is, as we all know, an extremely adaptable life-giving element. It collects wherever the terrain gives it an opportunity; it thunders down as a freshet over rocks or murmurs its way through woods and meadows; it reflects the sky and surrounding landscape in a still pool; and even the tiny puddles collecting in the ruts of a road or the furrows of a field can become an environment in which plants and creatures may live.

The following paragraphs present the pools and ponds found in nature, with brief descriptions of their particular characteristics.

Ponds—Lakes Without Depth

"A pond is a lake without depth," said the Swiss scientist François Alphonse Forel (1841–1912). Forel is considered the founder of limnology, that is, the scientific study of fresh waters. (*Limne* is the Greek word for pool or marshy lake.) Forel also noted a second characteristic of ponds, namely, that because of the shallowness of the water, higher aquatic plants that grow on the bottom may extend across the entire pond. Rarely deeper than 6 feet (2 m), a pond—unlike a lake—exhibits only minor temperature differences at various depths. Generally ponds are not large, often covering only a few square yards. One notable exception is the Neusiedler Lake on the Austro-Hungarian border that covers an area of 137 square miles (356 km^2) and, having an average depth of 4¼ feet (1.3 m), may be regarded as a giant pond.

Deadwaters—A Misnomer

Eddies, or what are sometimes called still or deadwaters, are found in rivers and streams wherever the current has been interrupted. Because the motion of the water is slowed, more plants and animals can establish themselves in such places than in faster-flowing waters. In these eddies, mosses and green algae may grow, the larvae of caddisflies enter their pupal stage, and predatory mayflies and fish lie in wait for prey.

In view of all this activity and life, the term *deadwaters*, which is sometimes used by people to describe these regions of streams or rivers, is clearly a misnomer.

Puddles—Small Bodies of Water Filled with Life

Puddles are usually only a couple of inches deep, and they are so-called periodic waters, meaning that they hold water only intermittently during a few weeks to at most a few months of the year. Puddles form for a variety of reasons; in the spring they are usually the result of melting snow; in the summer and fall they are likely to be caused by heavy rain or rising ground water.

Another feature of puddles is that no aquatic plants grow in them since they would not be able to survive the periods when the water dries up. Instead, regular terrestrial plants that can withstand short periods of being flooded are found in puddles.

In the pictures:
Above: The profligate ways of nature. One rarely sees such an abundance of flowering bladderwort as in this small pool in a lowland marsh.
Below: Tracks "on" the water. You can tell that there is a frozen pond beneath the snow only by the surrounding reeds and rushes.

A stretch of water in a wild wetland. A slight breeze is ruffling the water enclosed by reeds, rushes, and sedges and sets the water lilies dancing on the waves.

Puddles also have their own characteristic inhabitants: mainly single-celled organisms or protozoans, such as rhizopods and ciliates, and also lower forms of crustaceans or waterfleas. As long as there is water, these creatures multiply rapidly, and during dry spells they survive inside some sort of protective covering.

Artificial Ponds—Human Creations Claimed by Nature

The environment of an artificial pond is exactly like that of a natural pond, except for the fact that they are artificially created. Ponds made by humans are designed to serve certain ends, perhaps to hold fish or to store water for fighting fires. Unlike natural ponds, these ponds can be drained.

In earlier times almost every village in Europe had its pond, and over a hundred years ago a German school teacher by the name of

Friedrich Junge wrote a pamphlet entitled *The Village Pond as a Life Community,* in which he pleaded for teaching "experiential biology."

It is important to be aware that an artificially created pond that is no longer maintained will develop the fauna and flora characteristic of local natural ponds within a few years.

Quarry Pools—A Refuge for Flora and Fauna

Gravel pit and quarry pools come into being when sand and gravel or rock are removed and the resulting pits fill with ground water.

These bodies of water, which are permanent stillwaters, are today some of the most important surrogate biotopes (in Greek *bios* = life, *topos* = place), making up for rapidly disappearing wetlands and river islands and flood plains. The sand and gravel shores of quarry pools offer a dwelling place to many plants and animals.

The water of these pools supports fish and amphibians; water-loving plants spread along the moist margins; and the banks offer food and hiding places to insects and birds. And these water-filled pits have also become a source of recreation that we have come to take for granted. In the summer they are a popular alternative to public beaches.

Streams—An Ever-changing Encounter with Nature

A stream is water that is in constant flow. Consequently there has to be a gradient. Mountain streams arise high up and plunge toward the valley, hurrying along in V-shaped beds. At the other extreme are the lowland streams that, depending on the terrain, either wind their way through the landscape in many curves or flow lazily along a channel, digging it gradually deeper and deeper. The flow may be interrupted by waterfalls. Lowland streams have a U-shaped profile, usually with a sandy bottom and plants growing along the banks. This configuration has a cleansing effect on the water and also offers a plentiful supply of food (such as freshwater crustaceans) for many kinds of fish.

The fast-moving waters of mountain streams are refuge for brook trout, fish whose streamlined bodies are ideally adapted to this environment. But plants hardly have a chance to take root here. Lowland streams, on the other hand, carve hollows into their banks, and in these protected sites varied life forms thrive. It is especially in these pools and hollows that all kinds of plants and animals establish themselves.

Sad to say, but natural streams are becoming scarcer all the time; today, it is often difficult to find a lowland stream that still meanders along its natural course in lazy curves and has not been reduced to a straight ditch.

A *Nymphaea* hybrid named "Hermine." The petals of the blossom, which measures more than 6 inches (15 cm) across, are pure white. This water lily is very hardy and can be overwintered in the deepest part of a pool.

A water-lily pond in Bagatelle, near Paris. During the Baroque period, water was an integral part in the design of formal gardens for castles and mansions. The water was contained in strictly geometrical pools and rigidly straight channels. A natural-looking body of water grown over with water lilies would have been inconceivable at that time.

A swan with its young on a pond is a familiar sight in many parks.

Pond Models for Large and Small Gardens

Anyone thinking about setting up a garden pool with all the associated plant and animal life will quickly realize when researching the project that there are many different kinds of pools to choose from. To make the choice easier, the different pool types are described in this chapter. Possibilities range from natural-looking ponds at one extreme to ornamental pools with fish in them at the other and also include garden pools with a swimming area or marsh gardens whose special attraction lies in the interesting shapes and exquisite colors of the aquatic plants.

Many people think of a garden pool simply as a pool in a garden, with one pool differing from another simply in size, shape, and plantings. Often this perception is correct. But there are garden pools that are much more distinctive and have features that lend such a unique character to them that they deserve special names. Among these are the two most commonly built kinds of pools: the natural pond and the ornamental pool. People planning a pool often contemplate only these two types. But have you ever thought of the possibility of a koi pool, or of a pool that could double as a swimming pool, or of a play pool for children that could later be turned into a lavishly planted marsh bed?

Note: You will find detailed information on plants and animals mentioned in this chapter on pages 94–125. There are also basic instructions on how to build pools on pages 48–63. All important details concerning pool size and location as well as setting up lined pools and preformed pool shells are discussed.

A Natural Pond—Refuge for Native Flora and Fauna

Let us begin with the most natural of artificial pools, the so-called natural pond, which is like a piece of "pure nature" in a garden. Ecologists advocate this type of pool because it can become a home for many native plant and animal species whose natural habitat, the wetlands, is disappearing fast.

What You Should Know: Desirable as natural ponds may be, it is impossible to really duplicate nature. A natural pond in a garden is at best an approximation; it can never be a true substitute for the piece of nature that may be dying outside your garden. Still, any properly constructed naturelike pond is no doubt a worthwhile contribution to environmental protection.

There are several things you have to consider when you decide whether or not a naturelike pond is a possibility for your garden:

- The most fundamental principle is that once the pond is set up nature has to be allowed to take her course. You have to be willing to accept this. Only in a few rare situations should you step in and initiate corrective measures—if the pond is filling up and in danger of disappearing, for instance, or if the water is becoming too acidic, or if algae are taking over completely.
- A natural pond should be no smaller than about 160 square feet (15 m^2) or, preferably, 320 square feet (30 m^2), with a depth (deep-water zone) of at least 5 feet (1.5 m). An extended zone both of shallow water and of marshy ground is also important.

Play with water. This sculpture incorporates the movement of wind and water and requires plenty of space to produce its full effect.

- Technical devices such as pumps and pool filters are superfluous, and fountains and artificial lights are out of place here, as are stocked fish.
- Only if there are fields, meadows, shrubbery, and perhaps even wetlands nearby is it very likely that a plant and animal life resembling that found in natural waters will develop in your pond. You have to lower your expectations considerably—especially as far as animal life is concerned—if your garden is located in the city or in an industrial area or near highways or other roads with heavy traffic.

Location: Choose the quietest corner of your garden; five to six hours of sunshine are important for good plant growth.

Materials to Seal the Bottom: Pool liner; clay or clay tiles.

Plants: Use only native plant species. You can buy these at nurseries specializing in aquatic plants.

Some plants that do well in the marsh and shallow-water zones are: marsh marigold *(Caltha palustris)*, purple loosestrife *(Lythrum salicaria)*, bur reed *(Sparganium erectum)*, yellow flag or water iris *(Iris pseudacorus)*, cattail *(Typha latifolia)*, water plantain *(Alisma plantago-aquatica)*, arrowhead *(Sagittaria latifolia)*, and reeds *(Phragmites australis)*.

White water lilies *(Nymphaea alba)*, floating heart *(Nymphoides peltata)*, and water chestnut *(Trapa natans)* are suitable for deeper water (12 inches or 30 cm and deeper).

Purple loosestrife *(Lythrum salicaria)* adds a patch of beautiful color to the surroundings of a pool. The plant was used in earlier times as a folk remedy for its astringent properties.

Among plants that grow submerged on the water's bottom and play an important role in supplying oxygen are pondweed *(Potamogeton)*, common elodea or waterweed *(Elodea canadensis)*, and bladderwort *(Utricularia vulgaris)*.

Patient pond owners who are willing to let nature proceed at its own pace wait until plants appear by themselves, their seeds having been windblown or introduced by water birds.

Important: Do not dig up wild plants! Almost all aquatic and wetland plants are under protection (see HOW-TO pages 108–109).

Animals: Any creatures that turn up are welcome. In their search for waters to live and spawn in, frogs, toads, and newts may find their way to your natural pond. And almost inevitably dragonflies, diving beetles, water striders, water scavenger beetles, and whirligig beetles will also make their appearance.

Do not introduce any fish! If nature should "bestow" your pool with fish, you can generally leave them there. Fish do sometimes unexpectedly turn up in garden pools. This is because water birds may pick up sticky fish eggs on their legs or plumage. If the birds then land on your pond, these eggs may drop off, and sooner or later you will spot some young fish.

The Pond's Margin: Except for a small observation post, the rim of a natural pond should not be walked on. Simply work clay or clay tiles well into the soil along the edge of the pond and bury the pool liner in such a way that its edges stick up (see HOW-TO page 62). In the small area where foot traffic is allowed, it is best to put down a few natural rocks or an old log to protect the pond's edge. The surroundings of the pond should be planned to look as natural as possible. A garden of wild vegetation is ideal, but planting shrubs and flowering plants native to your area is also a step in the right direction. Plants suitable for the dry sections of the pond margin include smartweed *(Polygonum bistorta)*, yellow loosestrife *(Lysimachia vulgaris)*, blue moor-grass *(Molinia caerulea)*, and weeping sedge *(Carex pendula)*. The latter forms tufts among which you can easily create water holes for frogs (*Rana* species). There should also be some piles of stones and a heap of twigs mixed with leaves and compost nearby, as well as a mud puddle to supply building materials for swallow nests. And of course your compost pile can be nearby. The whole scene may have a romatically wild look. The only thing that is out of place here is a neatly groomed lawn. If one is already there, plant shrubs and bushes in it or let it gradually turn into a wildflower meadow near the water's edge.

Upkeep: Active maintenance is required only if the natural equilibrium of the pond is disturbed, as through excessive algae growth or if the pond is beginning to fill up with plants and decomposing organic material. If fish have become established and have multiplied in the pond, a deicer is helpful in the winter to aid the exchange of gases (see page 130).

A Miniature Natural Pond

This is essentially a smaller version of the natural pond just discussed. It is meant for the many gardens that are too small to accommodate a larger pool but whose owners would like to include as much of nature's variety as possible on their grounds.

What You Should Know: Because of the small size, you have to accept some compromises. The rule to follow here is: Leave nature alone as much as possible, but lend a helping hand by providing some regular maintenance.

- An area of at least 64 square feet (6 m^2) and a depth (deep-water zone) of at least 32 inches (80 cm) are recommended. The larger the pool is, the more animals will be attracted to it. Again an extended zone of shallow water and marshy ground is important.
- A small waterfall is helpful for providing oxygen, but a water fountain would be out of place here.
- You will need to install an air pump and in most cases a pool filter as well.

Location: The pond may be close to your house, but, for the sake of keeping the retreat of animal visitors relatively quiet and peaceful, the marshy area should not be right next to the children's playground.

Materials to Seal the Bottom: Pool liner, clay, clay tiles, preformed fiberglass shells are all suitable.

Flowers in bloom in and around a natural pond. Anyone planning a garden pool should include a marshy area next to it. There are great numbers of plants that thrive in wet ground, and many of them display the loveliest colors and shapes.

Plants: Native plants can be purchased at a nursery specializing in aquatic plants. Cultivated water lily varieties of the hardy type are a possibility.

Animals: Anything that chooses to settle in your pool. Within limits you may stock native fish, such as pumpkin seed or sunfish *(Lepomis gibbosus),* black bullheads *(Ameirus melos),* and bitterlings (see page 120). Brook sticklebacks will also be happy in a natural pool, but they can be a nuisance because they eat fish eggs. Water birds often introduce eggs of goldfish and carp. Fish that arrive this way can be left in the pond, but you should not stock goldfish.

The Pond's Margin: Shaping the margin in as natural a way as possible, with small bays, rock piles, and plants, will create the conditions wild visitors need. It is better if only a small portion of the shoreline will be walked on, and that stretch of the pond's edge should be reinforced with rocks or wood. For the dry areas near the pond, garden flowers, flowering shrubs, ferns, grasses, and ornamental perennials like rhododendrons and azaleas can be recommended and, of course, all the local wild plants.

Upkeep: In the fall all the plants that grow too vigorously should be thinned and detritus, filamentous algae (water net), and dead plant parts removed from the water with a blunt-tined rake. This noninterventive upkeep prevents harmful biological processes from getting started. If you live in a region with harsh winters you should cover the pool, especially if fish are to overwinter in it (see HOW-TO page 136).

Each type of pool has its own special characteristics. Once set up, a natural-looking pond should be largely left alone. With an ornamental pool, on the other hand, the aim is to regulate conditions with a judicious hand to assure the happy and healthy coexistence of plants and animals. If you want a goldfish or koi pool, the whole point is to show off the beauty of the fish to best advantage. In the case of a pool in which children will play, the challenge is to make it inviting for play and at the same time safe.

An Ornamental Pool

The most noteworthy quality of this kind of pool is its versatility, for an ornamental pool can be set up to accommodate not only stocked fish but wild visitors as well, creatures like frogs, dragonflies, and water striders. And there is not just one kind of fish that is appropriate. Pumpkin seed sunfish, chub, black bullheads, or bitterlings live in a well-tended ornamental pool just as happily as goldfish, golden orfes, and kois. Such a pool is also a wonderful place for the many beautiful cultivated varieties of water lilies.

What You Should Know: If the pool community of fish, plants, and visiting creatures is to thrive, some care has to be taken in setting up and maintaining the pool.

- The pool should have a minimum size of 65 square feet (6 m^2), and there should be a deep-water zone of about 10 square feet (1 m^2) that is at least 32 inches (80 cm) deep so that the fish can overwinter in the pool.
- Fish as well as wild visitors will thrive only if you proceed according to the motto: to each his rightful place. While the areas of open water will naturally be claimed by the fish, amphibians and other pool visitors need a different kind of environment. For them you have to create a fairly large marsh area that is fed water from the pool but is separated from it by a stone wall (see HOW-TO page 74). Many amphibians (like newts) prefer not to have fish close by and therefore need their own terrain, namely a shallow marshy strip next to the pool. This marshy part should be densely covered with vegetation and may dry up almost completely during the summer. Having this shallow zone also keeps goldfish from eating up all the eggs of amphibians.

A swimming pool with a wooden terrace. The terrace extends over the water, supported by pillars. The floating globular lights are connected to an underwater cable and use low-voltage electricity.

• A pool profile resembling that of a soup bowl with a flat rim is ideal but hard to realize in a very small pool. In order to end up with a shallow-water zone and an extended marshy area, at least part of the pool's bank has to be built somewhat steeper.

• Neither fish nor water lilies like to have water pouring down on them. It is therefore better to do without fountains that send jets of water high up into the air. However, something more modest, like a bubbler stone, a small fountain with a gentle splash, a spill pipe, or a tiny waterfall can be harmoniously incorporated into the overall design of an ornamental pool.

Location: Choose a spot where you spend most of your time and where the pool forms part of your view. The pool can be very close to your house, directly adjacent to a patio or terrace, for instance. Of course, any other spot in the garden is fine too, as long as it receives five to six hours of sunshine.

Even the smallest garden can be big enough. This pool, with its paved sitting area, is the focal point of a garden of only about 350 square yards (300 m^2). The mirrorlike surface of the water and the rich variety of plants around it create an enchanting harmony. The plastic duck decoys add another decorative touch.

At night and when the weather is cold, water lilies "go to sleep," that is, their flowers close up.

Materials to Seal the Bottom: Use either a pool liner or a preformed fiberglass shell.

Plants: Choose anything—from *Nymphaea* water lilies, floating hearts, water soldiers, and the yellow water lilies *(Nuphar lutea)* for the deeper area to the numerous marsh plants, like irises, lobelias, water plantain, purple loosestrife, and marsh marigolds, to name a few. There is much to pick from when you plant an ornamental pool with a shallow-water zone and a marshy zone. A survey of plants is provided on HOW-TO pages 108–109 to help you make appropriate selections.

Please keep in mind, though, that restraint is the mark of a master. Fish do not thrive in water that is shaded too much by water lilies, and many marsh plants are so prolific that they crowd each other out.

Animals: Since fish multiply in a pool that is well kept, restraint is called for here too. Also keep in mind the natural behavior of different kinds of fishes. Bitterlings, for instance, rely on mussels for "nurseries," and mussels need a sandy bottom. Sticklebacks are fierce predators that eat anything that moves—don't get more than two pairs. Goldfish come in many varieties, but not all of them are suitable for an ornamental pool (see the next section, A Goldfish Pool); the decorative veiltails, for instance, tend to present problems. Blunt-nosed minnows do well only in groups of at least five to nine fish. You will find more information on fish on pages 120–123.

The Pool's Margin: Anything that looks attractive is fine. Give your imagination free rein! Untreated wood and lime-free stone (pebbles, slate) can be used along the pool's edge in all kinds of ways. A full discussion of materials as well as suggestions for possible ways of arranging a pool's margin are found on pages 76–93. The photos, too, can give you some ideas. For example; if you do not have a patio near the pool, you can pave a small area and set up some garden furniture as shown in the photo on pages 24–25. This may produce an inviting spot for pleasant hours of relaxation.

Upkeep: Good filtration of the pool water is essential because uneaten food and the excreta of fish can quickly foul the water. You can filter the water with a special pool filter or, ideally, by circulating it through a stream which—if properly built—will act as a biological filter (see page 67). You also have to make sure there is enough oxygen in the water. For this you need an air pump.

Fall is the time for a thorough cleaning of the pool and for plant care in preparation for winter. In areas where temperatures may remain below freezing, small pools should have a deicer or be covered (see HOW-TO pages 136–137).

Bitterlings keep a pool clean. They like to eat insect larvae, including the larvae of mosquitoes. They also feed on blue-green algae.

Bitterlings deposit their eggs inside mussels. The young fish do not leave the shells until they measure about 1/4 to 1/3 of an inch (6–8 mm).

A Goldfish Pool

This kind of pool is especially designed for the needs of goldfish. Above all, the pool water has to be clean and well saturated with oxygen. If what you want are beautiful fish that are easy to look after, goldfish are the answer for you. These fish, which were first bred more than 1,000 years ago in China, are the most popular garden-pool fish today. If the fascinating breeds of goldfish appeal to you, a garden pool designed for goldfish will give you pleasure for a long time, for these fish can live for over 20 years and will also produce plenty of offspring.

What You Should Know: Goldfish are modest in their demands; the main prerequisite, as already mentioned, is clean water with a sufficiently high oxygen level.

- A pool size of 30 to 40 square feet (3–4 m^2) will do if the pool is equipped with a good filter and an air pump and if you practice moderation in stocking these prolific fish—three to six fish is plenty for a start.
- Goldfish need a deep-water zone of about 10 square feet (1 m^2) with 28 inches (70 cm) in depth for overwintering. In colder climates the depth should be 32 to 36 inches (80–90 cm). If a pool is less deep, the fish will have to overwinter in an aquarium.

Location: Choose a place as close to the house as possible. After all, you will want to be able to watch your goldfish; they also need to be fed—and who likes to run through a wet garden in rainy weather! The pool should receive sunshine about four to six hours a day. If there is too much sun, you can supply some shade by planting shrubs and tall perennials along the border. Water lilies also shade the water well. Although goldfish like sun-drenched shallow water, they also want to spend some time in the shade now and then.

Materials to Seal the Bottom: Flexible liners or preformed fiberglass shells can be used.

Plants: When planting a goldfish pool you can basically follow the rules that are given on page 22 for an ornamental pool. But it is a good idea to place the plants in the pool in containers (filled with a mixture of sand and clay). Cover the soil with a layer of plain sand. Goldfish like to burrow, and if they were to dig around in soil that contains clay—the kind of soil most plants need—the water would soon be murky and you would not see much of your beautiful fish.

Animals: The most reliable and hardy pond fish is the Common Goldfish *(Carassius auratus)*, which comes in reddish orange (the best known variety), brass color, bronze, white gold, and black gold. The fry are born blackish gray and do not take on their full adult coloring until about 3 months of age and sometimes not until the end of their second year, depending on the water temperature.

There are many varieties of goldfish. They differ from one another—often radically—in color as well as body and fin shape, but not all of them are suitable for keeping permanently in a garden pool. Apart from the common goldfish, the following varieties can be recommended:

- the Japanese fantail, or wakin, which comes in red, mottled red and white, and pure white. Its tail fins are slightly elongated.
- the red mottled calico or shubunkin, whose background color is white or sometimes blue, with red, yellow, black, and blue spots. The tail fin is elongated and veillike. Mottled shubunkins are born with almost complete adult coloring.
- the comet tail, which is usually a uniform red but can also be yellow, mottled red and white, or black. The tail fin is often longer than the body.

Important: The popular veiltails—they have double tails, which can be clearly seen when the fish are viewed from above—should be kept in a garden pool only during the summer; in the winter they should be moved into an aquarium. Breeds with long, trainlike fins or with shortened bodies are very slow swimmers and therefore fall prey to cats very easily. They are also subject to parasites and tend to have digestive problems. However, spending the summer in a

The comet tail is an attractive and unproblematic pool fish. It can even be left outdoors during winter.

The red-capped oranda is comfortable in a shallow (catproof!) pool only during the summer. Since it requires a water temperature of at least 64°F (18°C), it has to be moved into an aquarium for the winter.

A swarm of goldfish, the most popuar fish for an ornamental pool. Goldfish have enjoyed great popularity ever since they were first bred from silver carp in China about 1,000 years ago.

small pool 16 to 20 inches (40–50 cm) deep is beneficial for these fish. Just make sure the edge of the pool is shaped in a way that doesn't allow cats to get at the fish. One solution is to have square concrete or stone slabs that project over the water's edge (see HOW-TO pages 82–83).

The Pool's Margin: Let your own taste be your guide here. Examples to give you some ideas can be found on pages 76–93. What is important is that you have easy access to the pool for feeding the fish and for maintenance chores. For this reason you will probably want to have about half of the pool's edge covered with a surface you can walk on. A small waterfall, a bubbler stone, or some graceful small fountain looks attractive in a goldfish pool and supplies oxygen at the same time.

Upkeep: If you want to avoid oxygen depletion and dirty water you cannot do without technical devices in a small pond (up to 100 ft^2 or 10 m^2). You need a good filter and an air pump (see page 58). The devices must be kept in excellent working condition, and you should check every few days to make sure they are functioning perfectly. A stream is highly recommended to act as a biological filter (see page 67).

A Special Warning: Feeding goldfish is something adults as well as children love to do. It is fun to watch how quickly the fish learn to gather at the feeding place as soon as people appear. But don't give into these "hungry mouths" every time. Feed your goldfish sparingly, preferably twice a day, with special goldfish food, and never give them more than they polish off in a few minutes. Uneaten food has a deleterious effect on water quality, and you will have trouble keeping the water clean.

A Koi Pool

Japanese kois, an ornamental carp species, are fish that look particularly handsome in a garden pool because of their bright colors. Clear water is therefore essential, otherwise the beauty of these exotic fish is not fully visible. After a short acclimation period, kois become so tame that they let you touch them, and they even like to take food from people's hands. Kois recognize individual people by their gait and try in various ways to attract their attention, sticking the head out of the water, for instance, or begging for food by making loud eating noises, or practically turning somersaults in the air.

What You Should Know: These fish are not cheap, and setting up a pool to meet their needs adequately also runs into some money. Kois also grow big—up to 24 inches (60 cm)—and consequently need plenty of room. Two or three kois can easily be kept in a goldfish pond or an ornamental pool with other fish, but if you would like to keep a larger number you should offer these splendid animals a pool of their own, where they can really thrive.

- A koi pool should measure at least 100 square feet (10 m^2), or preferably 150 square feet (15 m^2). A deep-water area of about 10 square feet (1 m^2) and with a depth of 60 to 70 inches (1.5–1.8 m) is recommended if the fish are to overwinter in the pool.
- Kois have no need for a marshy zone, and any marsh area should, in fact, be separated from the pool by rocks or set up in a way that keeps the fish from swimming through it. But you should plan to have a marshy area all the same because water attracts all kinds of creatures that can find food and shelter only in a marshy environment.
- Clean, oxygen-rich water is essential for kois. Kois consume protein-rich food in considerable quantities and produce corresponding amounts of waste. Fish excretions have a negative impact on the water because they cannot be broken down through natural processes. That is why you need a good filter with as large a filter volume as possible and a powerful pump that turns over about 500 gallons (2,000 L) per hour. A coarse bio-filter material (no cotton wadding!) is recommended. You will also have to install an air pump (membrane pump) with an air stone (see page 58). The air pump should be left running continously all year around.

Brilliant color in the water:
Above, left: Shubunkin, calico goldfish.
Above, right: Ordinary goldfish, brass color and red.
Below: Kois.
All fish need clean water to thrive and to show off their colors and shapes to best advantage.

In the picture:
The lotus flower *(Nelumbo lutea)* is an exotic beauty that has adapted to a wide range of conditions in the United States and Southern Canada.

Location: Choose a partially shaded site (with five to six hours of sunshine) close to the house. Full sun should be avoided because it stimulates excessive algae growth, which makes it more difficult to keep the water clean.

Bottom Sealing Materials: Pool liners, preformed fiberglass shells of sufficient depth, or concrete poured by a professional contractor all are good bottom sealers.

Plants: Water lilies of all kinds are best, but they should be planted in containers (see HOW-TO page 104). With their big leaves water lilies help shade the water below them, and the underside of the leaves also removes large amounts of nutrients and carbon dioxide from the water. Algae are therefore unlikely to become a problem in the vicinity of water lilies.

Other floating plants that fit in well with water lilies are floating heart, water soldier *(Stratoites aloides)* and, especially, cattails *(Typha latifolia)*, which absorb a lot of organic waste materials.

Submerged plants like waterweed *(Elodea canadensis)* and pondweed *(Potamogeton)* are even more efficient at cleaning up waste materials than water lilies. They are planted in containers with a layer of pebbles on top of the soil so that the kois don't dig them up too quickly.

Animals: You can buy kois at pet stores or from dealers specializing in fish. The price depends on the quality of the breed and on the markings, especially those visible from above. These markings are supposed to be as symmetrical as possible. There are many different koi varieties that differ from one another in color and markings. Some are solidly colored in yellow, orange, silver, or gold; the multicolored strains include red-white-and-black, white-and-red, and blue-and-silver with a red dorsal stripe, to mention a few.

When you first stock a pool measuring 100 square feet (10 m^2), eight to ten juveniles are plenty because koi grow quite fast. A 1-year-old koi measures about 4 to 5 inches (10–13 cm), but by the time the fish is 3 years old it will have grown to about 14 inches (35 cm).

The Pool Margin: The pool's edge has to be cat-proof; otherwise, these trusting fish fall victim to felines all too easily. Shallow parts of the pool should be blocked off with rocks to keep the koi out so that cats tempted to catch them would be forced to get wet.

Except in the marshy area, you will want to have borders around the pool that you can walk on. Flagstones or concrete slabs extending about 8 inches (20 cm) beyond the water's edge are a good idea (see HOW-TO pages 82–83).

Upkeep: During the summer all that is required is feeding the fish and occasionally thinning plants that grow too profusely. The water quality should be checked regularly (see page 128) and, especially with small pools, a monthly water change is recommended (replace 30 percent of the water).

Ordinary goldfish or pond fish food is not adequate for kois, but pet food manufacturers also market special koi foods. If you want to offer your fish a special treat, you can give them pieces of beef heart (without gristle) soaked in a concentrated multivitamin solution.

In the summer it is best to feed koi fish several times a day, but only as much as they will eat up right away. When the water temperature drops to around 54°F (12°C) in the fall, stop feeding.

Transforming Your Swimming Pool into a Garden Pool

Many a poured-concrete swimming pool that was once the family's pride and joy now languishes unused in the back yard. Time-consuming maintenance, including draining the water and scrubbing the pool in the fall, and the realization that the chemicals indispensable for keeping the water clean are not good for one's skin or for the environment have led people to neglect their turquoise structures—in detriment to their yard's looks. In such a situation the thought of a garden pool with lovely plants begins to look more and more attractive.

The question then comes up whether it might not be possible to have a combination swimming pool/garden pool. This is, in fact, an idea that can be turned into reality without excessive labor and at moderate expense.

What You Should Know: There are two simple methods of turning a swimming pool into a garden pool.

1. If the basin is still intact, showing neither cracks or flaking paint, you can simply paint it grayish black or earth brown, using a waterproof paint. This creates the impression of a natural bottom. Then you set up a shallow section by partitioning some of the pool off with a wall of loosely piled rocks (see drawing, HOW-TO page 46).

2. If there are cracks in the concrete, the paint is flaking off, or some of the tiles in a tiled pool are loose, a liner is the answer. If there are concrete walls with a rough surface, it is a good idea to put a protective pad under the liner (available from pool supplies dealers or garden centers). Fasten the liner to the inside of the pool's edge with PVC-coated metal strips, pegs, and screws. After this first step, you continue as previously described under 1. Cover up the liner along the edge with plants in narrow, rectangular containers. One way to attach the containers is to hang them all

You cannot teach a cat not to go after fish. Goldfish and koi fall victim all too easily to the sharp claws of cats, the former because many of the highly bred varieties are unable to swim fast, and the latter because they are so trusting that they can be trained to become hand tame.

around the pool on the type of hooks used to support flower boxes on balconies.

Special Remarks: Plants and the occasional use of a pool filter will keep the water clean enough so that you can swim in it without worry. The chemicals you used to add to the pool water are no longer needed and would be harmful to the plants. The water is, of course, not chemically pure because all kinds of creatures are bound to invade the pool. Microscopic animals and small insects like water striders and water fleas are a natural part of a pool, and they, too, help keep the water clean because they "process" dead plant parts, algae, and other organic material. If you enjoy a swim in a wild pond or a quarry pool now and then, your pool in its new "natural" state will seem like pure heaven.

Plants: You can introduce many marsh and water plants into the shallow-water area. And If you don't mind swimming among plants, you can plant the deep part of the pool lavishly as well (place the plant containers on pillars built of perforated bricks). Just a few plants is fine, too, if you prefer it that way.

Animals: If you use your revamped pool only rarely for swimming, it can be an ideal home for goldfish or koi. The fish won't mind sharing the water with people now and then. A pool filter that works properly will keep the water clean enough and the oxygen level high enough for them. Generally, such a pool will be deep enough for the fish to overwinter in it.

The Pool's Margin: In most cases a swimming pool is surrounded by lawn. If that is what you like, you can keep it that way. But if you would prefer a somewhat more natural look, you can set up a marsh garden next to the pool (see page 38) or plant flowers, grasses, or ferns. Any kind of vegetation near the pool is fine.

Upkeep: The same maintenance chores are required as for other garden pools: thinning plants, replenishing water during prolonged dry spells, changing about a third of the water once or twice during the summer.

A vacation spent in your own backyard. Not at all an unpleasant prospect if you can relax next to the water in a lawn chair shaded by an umbrella. Chair and umbrella are set up on a wooden walkway that separates the swimming area from the rest of the pool. Dense pickerelweed plantings along the water add visual beauty to the scene.

A Garden Pool You Can Take a Dip in

If you are starting from scratch, you should plan for a steep bank on the side toward the house and on the opposite side a more gradual shore that will form a natural transition to the garden. An ideal depth for the swimming area is between 32 and 60 inches (80–150 cm).

What You Should Know: You can swim in a garden pool only if that area of the pool is separated from the so-called biotope area, namely, the area that serves as a plant and animal habitat.

• It is, of course, not necessary to seal off the two areas from each other completely, nor would this be desirable because the water you swim in is meant to benefit from the purifying effect plants and microscopic organisms have on the water. It is quite sufficient to separate the swimming area from the biotope area with a loosely piled rock wall or with L-shaped concrete blocks reaching up to about 8 inches (20 cm) below the water surface. Do not make the dividing wall any higher because you don't want to block the water exchange between the two areas.

• The division of the pool can be done in one of two ways:

1. If the edges of your pool are shallow all around, you can have a ring-shaped partition and swim in the center area. This way the entire marginal zone can serve as a biotope. The swimming area is reached by way of a wooden dock extending over the planted area.

2. Or you can divide the pool into two sections with the biotope area on one side and the swimming area on the other. Reserve one third of the pool for the biotope, and use the other two thirds for swimming. Here the swimming area is accessible from a section of shore that is not planted, or from a wooden foot bridge that leads all the way across the water (see photo, left-hand page).

• Here are other, somewhat more expensive ways of dividing the pool:

1. The part used for swimming can consist of a large, preformed fiberglass shell around which you can create a shallow shore area by putting down flexible liner at a gentle angle. This marginal area is then thickly planted with shallow-water and marsh plants.

2. A fiberglass shell to serve as swimming area may also be incorporated into an already existing pool, but this can be quite expensive.

Location: Place it anywhere in the garden. The site should get five to six hours of sun for the plants to thrive. If the pool receives less sun, use only shade-tolerant plants (see page 43).

Materials to Seal the Bottom: Use flexible liner with a nonslippery surface, clay, or a fiberglass shell combined with pool liner.

Plants: Reeds, bulrushes, cotton grass, purple loosestrife, buckbean, marsh marigolds, and many other shallow-water and marsh plants can be located in the biotope area. You may introduce a few water lilies and cattails in the swimming area, but do so sparingly.

Note: Many reeds have very sharp edges. Do not use these kinds. Ask a knowledgeable salesperson at a garden center for advice. Do not dig up reeds you find growing wild.

Animals: Beetles, dragonflies, and other insects will automatically move into the biotope area, and sometimes some amphibians appear as well. The larger the area, the more animals are likely to turn up. But don't expect too much! People swimming and splashing around in the water inevitably disturb the water in the entire pool, despite dividing structures. Unless the pool is very large, you should do without fish. In a pool measuring 400 square feet (40 m^2) or so, fish can get away from bathers.

The Pool's Margin: Wood and natural stone can be used; a paved area for sitting next to the swimming area is convenient; a small waterfall, a bubbler rock, or a small fountain all look nice; and flowering shrubs and various kinds of grasses can be planted around the water. A wooden dock can be set up to provide access to the swimming area. If you plan to cross the shallow marginal strip to get to the water, don't plant that section but fill it in with sand instead and be sure to glue some stones about the size of a baseball to the liner 20 inches (50 cm) or so below the water surface. These stones will keep the sand from sliding down and disappearing.

Upkeep: A good pool filter is useful, and it makes sense to change the water periodically (change about 30 percent of the water every six weeks during the summer). Turn the filter off while you swim. Leave the air pump on all the time (see page 58). In the fall a thorough cleanup is called for (see page 130).

The water iris or yellow flag *(Iris pseudacorus),* originally from the Old World, has become naturalized in the United States. In Europe it is now protected. You can buy many different cultivated varieties ranging in color from golden to light yellow and cream.

A Patio Pool

A patio pool brings water close to the house. Since you will be looking out on the water much of the time, this is the kind of pool where it makes sense to install some type of water fountain. A wide selection of devices that display moving water is available. You can also indulge your imagination when you plan the lighting for the pool. You can buy anything from underwater or floating pool lights to lanterns that can be strung along the pool's edge.

What You Should Know: Being able to step through a terrace door and stand next to a pool is a wonderful feeling. But remember that a pool this close to the house poses a danger not only to children but also to unsuspecting visitors who may not realize there is water at such close range. That is why lights are essential, especially at night when at least a small warning light should be kept on at all times. If there are young children around, you have to install a safety grate in the pool, as described on page 59. You will probably want to avoid a regular fence for aesthetic reasons; however, a wrought-iron fence can look quite attractive, particularly if it is embellished by climbing plants.

- The pool's size depends on the size of the patio; the depth can be anywhere up to 32 inches (80 cm).
- If flagstones or tiles have to be cut to size, this job should be left to a professional; the use of the cutting tools requires proper protective clothing (danger of flying sparks and fragments).

Materials to Seal the Bottom: Preformed shells are used because they are easiest to install. Before you remove the patio tiles or other type of flooring, trace the outline of the future pool exactly where it is going to be. Many manufacturers will supply patterns of the available shapes for this purpose. If you don't have a pattern to follow, place the shell on the ground with the opening at the top and trace the outline on the ground in chalk, using a two-by-four held vertically to guide you (hold a carpenter's level next to the two-by-four to make sure it is vertical). Then take up the tiling and excavate the hole (see Using a preformed shell, HOW-TO page 62). Now lower the shell into the hole. You can set the tiles back in place around the pool exactly where they were. If you don't want to cut them to fit along curves or corners, you can leave those areas, which are usually not very large, uncovered and plant them with bamboo or a ground cover. This gives the pool a very nice look.

Plants: You can have any marsh and aquatic plants you like in the pool. For the edge, choose any types of tub plants that fit aesthetically with what is growing in the water.

Animals: Goldfish, koi, or native fish can be kept in a patio pool, but if there are going to be fish, you will have to use a pool filter. To bring electricity and the air hose from the air pump to the pool, use protective PVC pipe (see page 56). Have the spaces between the patio tiles widened enough to accommodate the PVC pipe, and run the pipe to the power source. But both the electrical wiring and the stone cutting should be done by professionals!

The Pool's Margin: The patio setting will largely determine the design of the pool's edge. Decorative tiles or handsome stones around the pool can lend an especially elegant note.

Upkeep: Maintenance is the same as for other garden pools that require a thorough cleanup in the fall (see page 130).

With a pool located next to a terrace, special safety measures have to be taken. If there are small children around, a grate mounted below the water surface helps prevent accidents. In any case, illumination is called for, and lights should stay on all night.

A Play Pool for Children

All children love to splash around in the water, build sand castles, and set toy boats sailing. If you install a pool that offers these possibilities, you will have created a small paradise for them to play in.

What You Should Know: Do not plan the play pool too small.

- A play pool should measure at least about 30 to 40 square feet (3–4 m^2); otherwise it will soon get boring.
- The depth of the pool will depend on the age of your children. For very young children, 8 to 12 inches (20–30 cm) is sufficient; but the water should be no deeper than 16 inches (40 cm) even if the children are older (up to about 7 years of age) because of the danger of drowning.
- Never leave children near water unsupervised—that applies not just to babies and toddlers.
- The basin should have the same depth everywhere. Children slip easily on a slanted bottom and may hit their heads on the bottom or conceivably even drown.

Location: The pool should be in partial shade, or shade must be provided by an umbrella or awning. Children will otherwise get badly sunburnt if they spend hours splashing in the water.

Materials to Seal the Bottom: A thick liner (60 mils or 1.5 mm) with a nonslip surface, clay, or a preformed fiberglass shell with a slipproof bottom are all appropriate materials. If you use a liner, it is

Consistency of style. In the planning of this terrace pool emphasis was placed on the strict continuity of lines. The rectangular pattern of the vine-surrounded windows is repeated in the square pool with its light-colored edge and in the square shape of the trimmed box shrubs.

best to construct the pool edges of two layers of square beams, one on top of the other (see A Children's Play Pool, HOW-TO page 47). The resulting border provides both an ideal place to sit on and a surface for baking sand cakes.

Play Possibilities: Water all by itself does not make for a very interesting play pool. Fill the basin partially with sand, but only enough so that there are still about 4 inches (10 cm) of water. Add some stones of various sizes (ranging from golf ball to baseball size).

Plants and Animals: None.

The Pool's Margin: Grass or a low-growing, hardy ground cover that will withstand the traffic of children's feet can be planted.

Upkeep: Change the water frequently. Depending on how dirty the water is, scoop it out and replenish the pool with clean water. Do this in the morning, and don't let the children play in the pool until the water has warmed up again. They can catch cold even in the summer if they spend hours in cold water. Empty the pool completely for winter and scrub it thoroughly. Fill it with fresh, clean sand in the spring. Do not use any chemicals to keep the water clean!

Special Remark: A play pool that is no longer used by children can easily be transformed into a marsh bed. You might even want to set up a small splash fountain or a bubbler rock surrounded by stones (see drawing, HOW-TO page 47).

A Marsh Garden

Marsh marigolds *(Caltha palustris)* form thick cushions of deep yellow flowers. They bloom from April to June.

If you are primarily interested in aquatic plants you will derive a great deal of enjoyment from a marsh garden. Many plants thrive in places where the ground stays wet all year, and they come in the loveliest shapes and colors. Anyone building a pool should at the same time set up a marsh bed or garden near it because a marshy area not only supports beautiful plants but also offers an environment that is attractive to many animals.

What You Should Know: Since a separate marsh garden receives no water from a pool you have to check frequently to make sure the water level or soil moisture is still adequate.

- The size of the marsh garden depends entirely on your available space. The only thing that matters is that the entire excavated area be about 10 inches (25 cm) deep. Otherwise the marsh will dry out too quickly on hot days.
- Fill the marsh area either with earth from the bottom of the pool (the disadvantage of this method is that it is hard to check the moisture level of the soil) or simply put the plants, set in containers, in the marsh garden.

Location: A marsh garden can get full sun because most wetland plants do well in the sun; partial shade is fine too.

Materials to Seal the Bottom: Any somewhat large, shallow basin that holds water will do—a play pool that is no longer being used, a retired children's plastic splash basin, or a fiberglass shell. Flexible liner is inexpensive and very practical, but it has to be at least 40 mils (1 mm) thick because some aquatic plants (reeds) have roots strong enough to push through thinner liners. Pull the liner over rocks or square beams around the marsh bed's edges, making sure that the ends stick up. The ends of the liner have to stick up beyond the planned water level (or the surface of the marsh soil) or else the surrounding, drier earth will draw moisture out of the marsh garden.

Plants: The smaller a marsh bed is, the more you should avoid plants with a tendency to spread. Some plants that are well suited to a small area—less than 20 square feet (2 m^2) are marsh marigold *(Caltha palustris)*, water forget-me-not *(Myosotis palustris)*, Siberian iris *(Iris sibirica)*, bog arum *(Calla palustris)*, cotton grass *(Eriophorum angustifolium)*, golden club *(Orontium aquaticum)*, and, of course, dwarf cattails *(Typha minima)*, bur reed *(Sparganium erectum)*, and purple loosestrife *(Lythrum salicaria)*.

Different wetland plants require different kinds of soil. Some like soil that is alkaline while others prefer acid soil (containing peat). You can solve this problem by setting the plants into individual containers, each with the right kind of soil for the plants in it.

Animals: A marsh garden attracts many creatures. Just which insects, amphibians, and other animals will be drawn to your marsh depends on the rest of the garden and on the surrounding area.

The Margin: Natural, untreated wood, roots, and fieldstone always look nice in combination with plants.

Upkeep: Check the moisture level frequently and, if necessary, water with a garden hose. A marsh garden should never dry out completely. Plants that spread too vigorously have to be thinned now and then. In October, tall marsh plants should be cut back by nine-tenths. Spread the stems and leaves you have cut on the plants as insulation against freezing and wait until March before you throw them on the compost.

Glorious flowering. Aquatic plants thrive especially well in a marsh garden. Creeping Jenny with its penny-sized leaves and delicate yellow flowers is combined here with natural flagstones to form a truly lovely border.

The yellow pond lily *(Nuphar lutea),* also called brandy-bottle, thrives even in shady ponds.

A Duck Pond

The reason for building a duck pond is to have ducks in it. There is not much you can do here to achieve aesthetic effects with plants because the ducks will quickly pick them to pieces, and they also foul the water. Any vegetation for such a pond has to be very robust to survive.

What You Should Know: The pond has to be large enough to accommodate at least one pair of dwarf ducks.

- A size of at least 130 square feet (12 m^2) is required.
- Pour enough sand into the pond to make a 2-inch (5 cm) layer on the bottom.
- There has to be a small island (about 3 feet or 1 m in diameter) in the pond. Such an island can be constructed easily with the help of a U-shaped concrete block (available at building supply stores) and a shallow plastic basin. Suitable basins are available form manufacturers of preformed pool shells (see drawing, HOW-TO page 46).
- Place a small duck house made of wood on the island.

Materials to Seal the Bottom: Use a pool liner, clay, or a concrete basin (built by a professional contractor).

Plants: Place broad-leafed cattails *(Typha latifolia),* and yellow pond lilies *(Nuphar lutea)* in containers next to the island. In the shallow-water zone you can plant yellow flag *(Iris pseudacorus)* and reeds *(Phragmites australis).* It is better not to attempt other plantings because the ducks would eat everything bare in no time. Let grass grow down to the edge of the water. If you want to provide a special treat for your ducks, plant some nettles along the pond's edge or nearby; ducks love to eat the shoots, which are high in vitamins.

Animals: None, since they wouldn't survive long.

Upkeep: To keep the water tolerably clean, about half should be changed every month. In the winter the air pump, which supplies the water with oxygen, has to be kept running constantly so that the pond won't freeze over completely. Pump the pond dry in the spring and completely remove the detritus.

Note: If you want to know more about keeping ducks, consult the specialized literature mentioned in the back (see page 143).

Other Pool Ideas for Special Situations

Many gardens at first glance do not seem to offer a good prospect for setting up a pool. But before you give up on the idea, look over the following sections to see if one of the special cases described offers a solution for your particular situation.

A Pool on a Hillside

The important thing with a pool located on a slope is to make sure there are no earth slides. The use of L-shaped concrete blocks (available from building supply centers) will keep the pool and surrounding earth in place. Dig away the slope about 28 inches (70 cm) deep and line the L-shaped blocks up next to each other. When you put the flexible liner down, it is best to glue it directly to the blocks with a silicone binder and weigh it down with perforated bricks or stones. The downhill side will be secure if you set wooden posts in a founda-

Previous double page:
Water as the basic theme. If you want to lend an unusual quality to your garden, plan to turn it into a water garden with several pools. A private garden of average size is generally large enough to accommodate two pools and a marsh bed. One pool could be for fish, the other primarily for plants.

tion of ready-mix concrete. To fasten the liner around the edge, wrap it around laths which are then nailed to the top of the posts (for more detailed instructions, see HOW-TO page 46).

Raised Pools for Quick Construction

Hard, rocky ground sometimes makes it impossible to dig deep enough for a pool. If you are reluctant to resort to a pneumatic hammer, you can build a raised pool. A raised pool is also a good answer for people who have little desire for digging big holes.

Mark the intended pool outline, and also mark the deep-water zone. Then dig posts into the ground along the edge of the pool. The posts should stick up into the air a good 16 inches (40 cm). Then dig a hole for the deep-water zone (generally an area of about 10 ft^2 or 1 m^2), piling up the earth you have excavated behind the posts, where plants can be planted later. Cover the entire pool area with flexible liner, and nail the edge of the liner to the posts. Since you will put the plants to be placed in the pool in containers, there is no need for earth on the bottom. If the pool is large enough (50–60 ft^2 or 5–6 m^2), you can even have fish in it.

Sweet flag or calamus *(Acorus calamus)* was formerly cultivated for its pharmaceutical properties. Sweet flag does best in the shallow water of a marshy area.

A Pool in the Shade

Many garden owners assume that they cannot have an attractively planted pool in a garden shaded by trees. They have come to believe this because they have often read and heard it said that pool plants need a lot of sun. Although that is true on the whole, more plants than you might think do well in and around a shady pool. Rhododendrons and azaleas, for instance, thrive beautifully in the damp air and moist soil found near a pool and add lovely colors to the surrounding landscape. Rich shades of green and interesting fall colors are provided by the many different kinds of ferns.

In the shallow area, marsh marigold *(Caltha palustris)*, bog arum *(Calla palustris)*, mare's tales *(Hippuris vulgaris)*, yellow flag *(Iris pseudacorus)*, creeping Jenny *(Lysimachia nummularia)*, globeflower *(Trollius europaeus)*, and brooklime *(Veronica beccabunga)* will grow well. Sweet flag *(Acorus calamus* or *A. gramineus)* and yellow pond lily *(Nuphar lutea)* like the deeper water. However, the popular *Nyphaea* water lilies do not do well in the shade.

Wildlife will be attracted by a shaded pool just as much as by a sunny one. The more natural the surrounding landscape, the greater the likelihood that frogs, toads, salamanders, and newts will make their appearance, not to mention innumerable insects.

Garden Puddles

Puddles are the answer not only for very small gardens but also for nature lovers who would like to observe the small animal life that flourishes in water.

A garden puddle is best made of clay. Clay is the most natural material for this purpose, and not much of it is needed. An area of 20 by 60 inches (50 x 150 cm) with a depth of just a couple of inches is sufficient, for the characteristic feature of a puddle is that it is not permanently wet, being filled with water at most a few months of the year. Of course, you can also choose to put down pool liner to hold the water for your puddle. Plant the puddle with rock cress, creeping brooklime, forget-me-nots, and horsetails. Toads, frogs, dragonfly larvae, and other tiny creatures will inevitably turn up.

Above left: Plains leopard frog *(Rana blairi)*.
Below left: Bullfrog *(Rana catesbeiana)*.
Right: Green tree frog *(Hyla cinera)*.

Water Gardens

Garden pools are often called water gardens. The two terms have become somewhat interchangeable. But if we look at water gardens from the point of view of landscape design, we can define the term more precisely and say that a water garden is a garden (or a part of a larger landscaped area) where water is a predominant feature. There are many examples of water gardens. Leaving aside the gardens of antiquity, like those of Rome, we think immediately of English gardens, whose special quality derives from the presence of pools, streams, waterfalls, and fountains of all kinds. Not all of these gardens are huge parks surrounding splendid castles; sometimes they are private gardens, often of quite modest proportions.

Perhaps you, too, are intrigued by the idea of creating a special effect in your garden by turning it into a water garden. You will find the individual elements that go into the making of such a garden in this book: The descriptions and photos of model pools, of running streams, various kinds of water fountains, and of beautiful plants offer plenty of suggestions, so that you will surely be able to "compose" your own version of a water garden. All you need to start with is paper and a pencil so that you can draw a plan. The beginning point is a pool that either exists already or is planned as the centerpiece. A stream will function as a link to everything else (see page 66).

The simplest model of a water garden, one that can be realized even in a small garden, consists of a pool, from which a stream winds through the garden. Water is supplied by an artificial spring (bubbler stone or a waterfall, see drawing in HOW-TO page 93).

Above, left: American toad *(Bufo americanus).*
Above, right: Rough skinned newt *(Taricha granulosa).*
Below, left: Southern toad *(Bufo terrestris terrestris).*
Below, center: Giant or marine toad *(Bufo marinus).*
Below, right: Red-spotted newt *(Notophthalamus viridescens viridescens).*

More expensive to build are water gardens made up of several pools, all connected to one another, and perhaps including various waterworks. This requires more complicated planning to make sure water will be channeled to all the places where it will be needed. If there is a long enough stream, it can connect a goldfish pond, a pool designed just for swimming, and a small natural pool. Of course, you could have two or more unconnected pools, but then the fascination and the filtering effect of a running stream are missing. Elaborate water gardens of this kind are best realized on a large piece of property.

A precise plan of the entire garden is important because water plays such a predominant role in it. Keep in mind the following points in your planning:

- Since the plants of the garden, the pools, and the stream should combine to create a harmonious whole, you have to have an overall planting plan.
- It is a good idea to coordinate the flowering seasons of the different plants in such a way that something is in bloom in and along the water all summer long and that there are some vibrant colors in the fall, too.
- When you select the hues of the flowers, let your taste and feelings guide you, almost as though you were a painter. Harmony is what you want to achieve, and sharp color contrasts are best avoided. You may even want to restrict yourself to different shades of the same color for entire areas.

HOW-TO: Pond Models

Instructions, Advice, and Solutions to Problems

On these HOW-TO pages you will find examples of how to construct several types of pools.

A Raised Pool

Drawing 1

This kind of pool is an especially good solution for places where it is impossible, because of the soil consistency, to dig a sufficiently deep hole. Mark the outline of the desired pool and also the deep-water zone, then excavate the latter area to a depth of 14 inches (35 cm). Dig posts about 32 inches (80 cm) long into the ground along the outline of the pool, letting them stick out into the air 16 inches (40 cm). Mound the excavated soil up behind the posts. Position flexible liner in the pool area and nail the ends to the posts. Then plant the mounded earth with plants that will put out plenty of roots to hold the soil in place. If some of the border around the pool is to be walked on, reinforce that section with a wall of loose rock.

A Duck Island

Drawing 2

If there is an island, it will quickly become your ducks' favorite spot on the pond. A duck island is simple to build: Submerge a U-shaped concrete block (available from building supply centers) where the water is about 32 inches (80 cm) deep. To prevent abrasion or tearing of the pool liner it is necessary to put one or two thicknesses of extra liner and a protective pad under the block. Then set a shallow plastic tub (about 8 inches or 20 cm deep and about 3 feet (or 1 m in diameter) on top of the block. The edge of the tub should be slightly above the water level. Fill with fist-sized rocks, and cover with pieces of sod.

A Pool for Swimming

Drawing 3

The simplest way of separating the swimming area from the planted section in a garden pool or a converted swimming pool is to build a stone wall. Pile the stones (irregularly shaped fieldstones are best) the same way as if you were building a loose-rock wall, but cement the stones together with dabs of silicone glue to make sure the wall will be steady. Do not mortar the stones together because the water must be able to pass back and forth between the stones. Partially fill in the area behind the wall with dirt (a mixture of sand and clay), and plant aquatic plants either directly on the bottom or in containers.

As support for a dock place two U-shaped blocks on the bottom with the ends pointing upward. Be sure to put extra pieces of liner and pads under the blocks. Then set the ends of the posts that support the dock into the U-shaped blocks and pour ready-mix cement around them. To increase stability, nail two boards crosswise to the posts. Using rust-proof nails or screws, attach two crossbeams to the posts, then nail the deck boards to the crossbeams.

1. A raised pool is an ideal solution for a garden with rocky ground.

2. A duck island used by the birds as a refuge for resting and breeding.

3. A garden pool where you can also take a dip. If you would like to be able to swim in your garden pool or would like to transform your swimming pool into a garden pool that offers the opportunity for a swim, plan to separate the bathing area from the section that will have plants and animals in it.

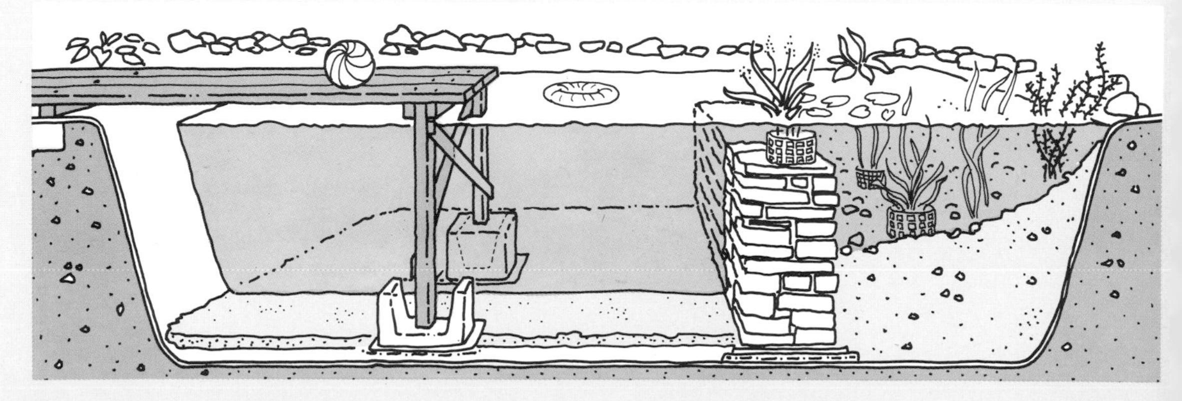

4. A pool on a slope. The uphill side has to be reinforced so that there is no danger of earth slides, and the downhill wall has to be strong enough to withstand the pressure of the water.

5. A play pool for children. All you need for this is some square beams and a strong flexible liner (60 mils or 1.5 mm).

A Pool on a Hillside

Drawing 4

Dig into the hillside about 28 inches (70 cm) deep. Then place a row of L-shaped concrete blocks (available from building supply centers) along the uphill side of the pool to keep the earth from sliding down. (The short end of the L points into the hill.) Fill in behind the blocks with dirt and large and small stones (building a kind of retaining wall as shown in illustration 4. Secure the downhill side with another row of L-blocks, the short ends pointing away from the hill. For a firm base, put some fairly big stones underneath the L-blocks. Place the flexible liner in the pool cavity you have thus created, and weigh down the liner ends along the L-blocks with stones or plant containers. Glue the liner to the L-blocks with silicone glue or pull it over the blocks and bury the ends.

To cover up the L-blocks on the downhill side, fill in with dirt or, better yet, pile up flat rocks to form a wall in steps ascending up to a plank that is mounted on top of the blocks.

A Children's Play Pool

Drawing 5

A square or rectangular play pool is easiest to build. About 30 to 40 square feet (3–4 m^2) is a good size. Dig away enough earth so that the depth of the hole plus the thickness of one square beam (these are between 6 and 8 inches or 15 and 20 cm thick) add up to no more than 16 inches (40 cm). The excavation should be the same depth all over. For the edge you will need two layers of square beams. Place the first layer and fasten the beams to each other at the corners with angle irons. Put down a protective pad and the flexible liner, pull them across the wood, and nail them to the wood. A second layer of beams is also held together with angle irons at the corners. The top beams are fastened to the bottom ones with wood screws. Add enough sand to the basin to leave room for only about 4 inches (10 cm) of water.

A Separate Marsh Bed

Drawing 6

A marsh bed is set up exactly like a children's play pool (see drawing 5), or you can convert an unused play pool into a marsh bed. Fill the area with soil from the garden pool. Place plants in this soil or in containers. Keep the soil moist!

A Small Pool for a Fountain

Drawing 7

Small pools are also set up like a play pool (see drawing 5). Here, however, you need electricity, and the wiring for it should be installed by a licensed electrician. Make piles of perforated bricks in the pool that reach just to below the liner edge (the top of the first layer of beams); place the pump with the appropriate fittings (a small spray or splash fountain, a water wheel, or a dome fountain) in the basin. You will then need a steel grate just slightly smaller than the pool; lay it horizontally on the piles of perforated bricks and cover it with fairly large stones.

6. A separate marsh bed. The bed is lined with pool liner and bordered with square beams just like a children's play pool. Plants can be set into the soil or into containers.

7. A water basin with a decorative fountain. This is a good way of recycling an old children's play pool that is no longer being used.

Building a Pool Made Easy

A number of factors must be taken into account when planning a pool. The location will depend largely on what your expectations of a pool are. Size is determined by how much space is available. The choice of an exact site is affected by the nature of the ground (you probably don't want to dynamite away rocks) as well as by the presence of trees (falling leaves and needles adversely affect water quality).

Whatever kind of pool you want to build—whether you intend to follow one of the models described in the previous pages or revamp an existing garden pool—you will do better if you know the basics of construction. Quite a few details require careful thought, from choosing the site to installing wiring and plumbing. You should also know how to work with the various materials used to seal the bottom of the pool. All this information and anything else you need to know you will find in the following pages, particularly on the HOW-TO pages with their instructive drawings.

Careful Planning—The Quickest Way to Success

It is well worth your time to start out by drawing the pool you envision on paper in full detail. Remember that mistakes in construction can be corrected only at great cost in time and money.

What to Consider When Choosing a Site

You have no doubt read more than once that a pool should fit harmoniously into the garden around it. This obviously makes sense, but each individual garden is different enough to make it impossible to give general rules for achieving this harmony. So let us approach the problem from the practical side. Look at your garden and ask yourself what your expectations are. Do you want to look out on the water as much as possible? Then the pool should be within easy sight of the place where you spend most of your leisure time (the patio, or a spot of the garden where you like to sit and relax). If, on the other hand, you want a natural pool, it should be in the quietest corner of the garden.

Once you have settled this basic question, take a closer look at the chosen location with the following points in mind:

Location: Five to six hours of sunshine are ideal for a pool. This means that it should be partially shaded, probably with an east or west exposure. If the place gets sunshine all day, that is, if it has a southerly exposure, you should plan on providing some shade by planting tall-growing grasses, bushes, or ornamental shrubs, for instance. A dense cover of water lilies also shades the water well. Small pools, especially, need sun alternating with shade. The sun stimulates plant growth, and shade is necessary during hot spells to keep the water from turning into a warm, oxygen-depleted brew where algae can quickly get out of hand.

Effects of Weather: Most of the cold weather comes out of the north and northwest—as the expression "icy north winds" suggests. That is why these sides of the pool should be protected. If your house or existing plantings do not already act as a wind break, you will need room for marginal plants that grow 16 to 20 inches (40–50 cm) tall. Evergreen hedges, such as privet, offer good protection against wind and weather especially in the cold part of the year. A raised berm is also a possibility. You can use dirt excavated in building the pool for this.

Trees Near the Pool: Trees provide shade, but their foliage creates a problem particularly in the fall, because the leaves that drop into the pool can affect the water quality in a way that threatens pool life. The tannin released by decaying leaves quickly raises the pH of the water. If you choose or are forced to locate the pool close to trees, you have to either remove the leaves from the water or spread a net over the pool (use a bird net, available at garden centers).

Big or Small?

This question, which presents itself to just about anyone who contemplates building a pool, is not easy to answer. We cannot give a minimum size that applies to all situations because the size of a pool depends on many factors. Among them are the size of your garden, how much effort and money you are willing to invest, and—very important—your own desires and expectations (fish, bathing, or natural look and conditions).

And you must be sure to take into account the "biological balance" of the pool. You will encounter this concept not just in connection with the size of a pool. The goal of all your efforts in setting up your pool, planting it, and providing upkeep is to achieve and maintain the biological balance. All this really means is that there has to be a balance between *producers*, that is, organisms that supply nutrients (dead plant parts and animals), and *consumers* (living plants as well as plant- and meat-eating animals). If there are more nutrients than are being used up, the water quality deteriorates. In extreme cases, the pool can become eutrophic. The result is excessive growth of algae, which in turn causes a big drop in the oxygen content of the water. If nothing is done, even the algae die, and all pool life, both plant and animal, comes to an end.

A biological balance is more difficult to achieve and maintain in a small pool than in a larger one.

When deciding the size of the pool, remember that some useful practical conclusions can be drawn from the biological interconnections described above:

- In a small pool that is to accommodate fish, other animals, and plants a biological balance can usually be maintained only with the help of technical devices, some work on your part, and regular checking of the water quality. This is because small amounts of water react quickly to external influences. An overload of nutrients caused by dropping foliage, a breakdown of the pool filter or the pump, fertilizer runoff from the lawn, and so on can ruin the water quality in no time. If you do not promptly step in to restore proper conditions, you may find your fish floating belly up.
- The larger the pond, the longer it will take for the biological balance to be upset, assuming, of course, that the pond is planned properly and contains plenty of different kinds of plants.

A Japanese stone lantern lends style to this koi pool. Such ornaments are sold in various designs and sizes.

Getting across without getting your feet wet. The concrete footing for the heavy natural rocks serving as stepping stones was constructed by a professional builder.

Depth of the Water: Specific suggestions are given in the descriptions of different pond models. As a general rule, a pool should include three different ecological areas, each of which is important for plant and animal life, namely, a marshy zone (up to about 10 inches or 25 cm deep), a shallow zone (10–20 inches or 25–50 cm deep), and a deep-water zone (over 20 inches or 50 cm deep). If fish are to overwinter in the pond, there has to be an area of 10 square feet (1 m^2) that is 28 inches (70 cm) deep or more, depending on the situation.

The Shape of the Pool

Choose the shape that is most aesthetically pleasing to you and that, in your opinion, looks best in the context of your garden. You can lay down a garden hose or a long rope in the planned shape to see how the pool would look.

Keep in mind that curves and shapes with many angles make excavation and sealing of the bottom harder and more expensive. Complicated shapes take more pool liner, and if you are contemplating a preformed shell, even something as simple as an L-shape is more expensive than a plain round or oval shell.

What to Do with the Soil

This is a question you should give some thought to at the planning stage. Since you cannot, generally, use the excavated material for the bottom of the pool—the soil is usually too rich—you have to decide whether you will have to have it carted away or if you can use it in your garden. Perhaps you can use it for a berm on the pool's north side, for a rock garden, or for constructing a waterfall. There are many ways to use soil in a garden, but you have to think about where you are going to put it until you are able to use it or have it carted away. If it is going to be piled even briefly on your lawn, put down big plastic sheets first, or your lawn will suffer.

This rhododendron hybrid retains its brightness of color from the time the flowers open until they wilt.

Sealing Materials

Decide during the planning phase which material you are going to use to seal your pool.

Flexible Liners and Preformed Fiberglass Shells: Liners and shells are the most commonly used ways to hold water. Both materials can be used by people without much building experience. You will find detailed instructions on the HOW-TO pages 62–63.

Clay: The material preferred by many who want a natural-looking pond is clay. But clay is not easy to work with. It is sold by building supply firms, but in some places it is not readily available.

The hole dug for the pool has to be covered with a layer of clay about 12 inches (30 cm) thick. Spread the dry, crumbly clay evenly and then wet it. Knead the water into the clay with your feet or with a mason's trowel. You want to end up with a layer of clay that is evenly thick. Add about 4 inches (10 cm) of sand on top of the clay so that the clay will not be stirred up later by animals and cloud the water. Finally, fill the pool slowly with water. At first some water may ooze away, but this will stop as the cracks fill with mud.

You will need less clay if you first line the bottom with unfired brick (available from brick factories).

Water and Electricity for the Pool

You should plan on having water and electricity available close to the pool, even if you do not expect to use technical equipment, like filters and centrifugal pumps. In a couple of years you will inevitably get tired of running the garden hose and an electric cable for the water pump to the pool for the necessary water changes.

Water Supply: The simplest method is to run a solid garden hose, buried about a foot deep in the ground, from the water source to the pool. To prevent damaging the hose later on, mark the water line and take a picture of it or enter its course on a plan drawn carefully to scale. A more expensive method is to have a plumber install a water outlet next to the pool.

HOW-TO: Building a Pool

What Anyone Building a Pool Should Know

No matter what building material you are planning to use, there are some basic matters you have to decide. Among them are not only the choice of an appropriate site but also whether special measures to provide safety for children have to be taken and whether a drain will be necessary.

Choosing the Site and Planning the Shape of the Pool

Drawing 1

Sun, the source of light and warmth, is important for good plant growth, but so is shade. The pool should therefore have at least five to six hours of direct sun. If the pool is exposed to the sun all day, you have to provide shade by planting tall grasses, shrubs, or bushes around the edge. A dense planting of water lilies will also shade the water. Remember that only certain plants do well in and around pools that lie in the shade (see A Pool in the Shade, page 43).

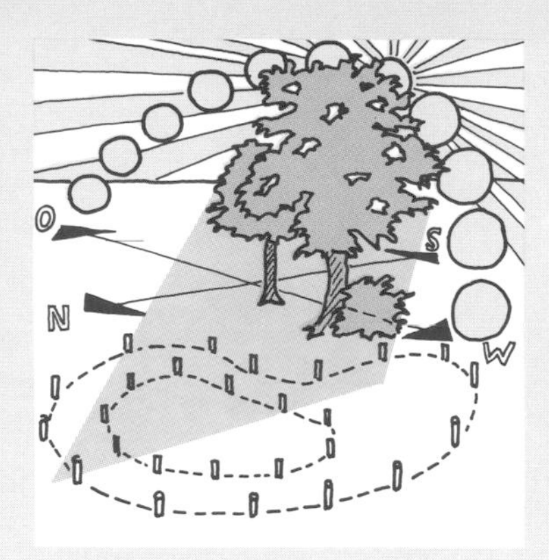

1. Note how many hours the sun shines on the selected site, then mark the outline of the planned pool with wooden pegs; also mark the deep-water zone.

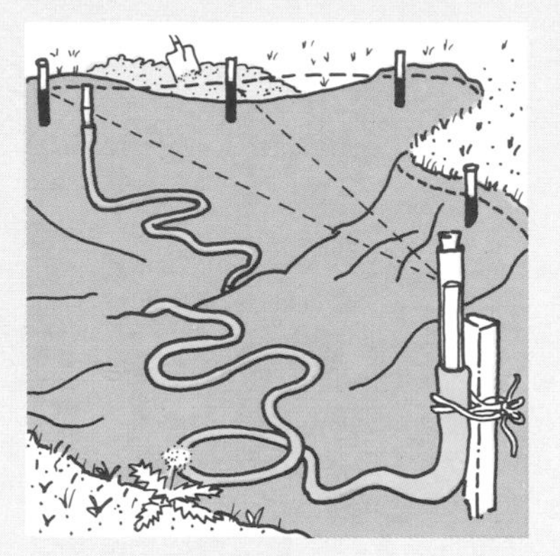

2. Excavate the pool cavity and check with a hose level if the edge is at an even height all around; if not, adjust it to make it level.

Once the site has been chosen, tap wooden pegs into the ground along the planned outline. To make sure that the deep-water zone will not be too big or too small and that it will be dug in the right place, mark its outline too, in the same way.

Adjusting the Edges for Height

Drawing 2

When the hole for the pool has been excavated, you have to check the edges for evenness. The edge has to be absolutely level all around, or else the water will spill out of the pool like soup from a bowl that is set down at a tilt. A hose level is the tool for this job. A piece of ordinary garden hose can be converted into a hose level as follows. Stick a piece of clear plastic tubing in each end of the hose and fill the hose with water. Tie one end to a post pounded into the ground in the excavated area and pick up the other end. Walk along the pool's perimeter and mark the water level on the pegs that outline the pool's shape. Correct the height of the pool's edge by removing and filling in dirt as needed.

3. A pool that will have plants and animals living in it should be planned to have four different habitats: a marshy zone, a shallow-water zone, a water-lily zone, and a deep-water zone.

4. Special safety precautions must be taken to protect children against accidents. One good safety device is a solid metal grate installed about 4 inches (10 cm) below the water's surface.

Different Habitats in the Pool
Drawing 3
What is meant here by habitats are zones of different water depth. A variety of depths is necessary both to accommodate different kinds of aquatic plants and to provide favorable living conditions for various animals. The necessary variety is achieved if the pool's profile is in the form of steps or if the pool has the shape of a soup bowl with a wide rim, that is, a deep bowl with a gently sloped edge.

To give an example: The marginal, marshy area is covered with 0 to 6 inches (0–15 cm) of water. For plants that do not mind standing in water, fill in 4 inches (10 cm) of soil. For those that do not flourish in water, soil is added up to the top. The next level, the shallow-water zone, can be up to 12 inches (30 cm) deep. Adjacent to it is the water-lily area with up to 24 inches (60 cm) of water. Finally, the deep-water zone of pools with fish living in them should be at least 28 inches (70 cm) deep.

You can prevent the soil from sliding to the next lower level by separating the different zones with walls of rocks.

The Safety Grate in the Pool
Drawing 4
A grate in the pool is a practical and nearly invisible safety device for the protection of children. You will need a grate of welded steel that is either galvanized or plastic coated (mesh size 2–4 inches or 6–10 cm). The grate is laid on piles of perforated bricks. Pile the bricks high enough for the grate to rest on them horizontally about 4 inches (10 cm) below the water's surface. Make sure the supports are solid; it would be disastrous if the grate tipped over when weight is placed on one end of it.

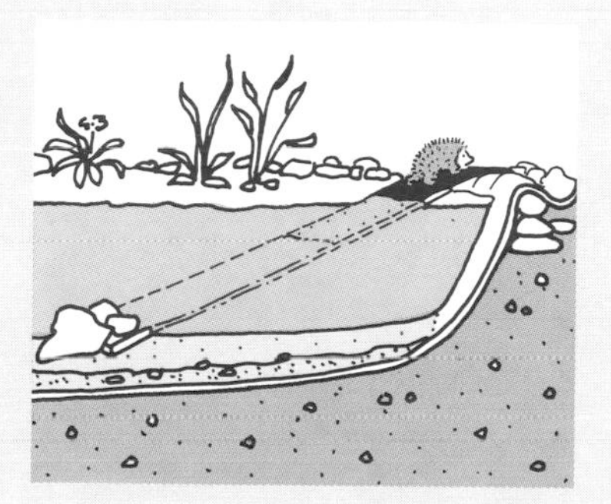

5. If the bank is steep, a board is needed to help animals that have fallen into the pool climb back out.

An Escape Route for Animals
Drawing 5
A long board sticking into the pool at an angle will help animals climb out of the water. To keep the board from sliding all the way into the pool the lower end should be weighed down with rocks. Nail a piece of liner about 20 inches (50 cm) long to the upper end and glue it to the edge of the pool liner (with silicone glue), or bury it in the ground along with the pool liner.

A Drainage Pit
Drawings 6 and 7
A drain or a spillway will keep the pool from flooding after prolonged rains. You can set up a drainage pit quickly and easily with the help of a wire compost bin (available at garden centers). Dig a hole big enough to accommodate the bin, cover the walls (not the bottom!) with flexible liner, and fill the bin with fist-sized rocks.

You can use a piece of roof gutter to connect the pool to the drainage pit. Another possibility is to dig a shallow trench, line it with plastic so that it forms a nonleaking channel, and fill it with rocks, so that young fish are not swept out of the pool and into the pit.

6. Drainage pits have proved very effective for taking care of excess water.

7. A gutter is filled with coarse gravel or pebbles.

Charm and beauty achieved by combining plants, water, and stone. Bricks, laid on their sides, and steps leading down to the pool help break the rigidity of straight lines. The lilies of the Nile *(Agapanthus)* are planted in tubs, where they look very handsome. Some of the terrace tiles had to be removed to plant the box shrubs, which are trimmed to spherical shape.

A robin taking its morning bath.

Electricity: Here no inexpensive solution can be recommended in good conscience. You have to hire a licensed electrician to do the wiring for bringing electricity to the pool and to install the outlets needed for the electrical equipment. These receptacles must have the GFI (Ground Fault Interrupter) safety feature that automatically stops the flow of electricity should an accidental surge of electricity discharge into the pool water. All you can do yourself is to lay a pipe (for instance, a 1-inch PVC pipe) to run the wires through. Dig a trench for the pipe about the depth of a spade and at a slightly downhill angle from the house. This way the pipe will be a little lower toward the pond so that any moisture inside it will drain away from the house.

Since an air pump (diaphragm pump for supplying oxygen) is indispensable—especially for pools with fish—you should lay down a second PVC pipe for running the air hose for the pump from the house to the pool (see page 58).

Preventing Accidents Caused by Electricity

Be sure to observe the following safety rules:

- Wiring may be installed only by a licensed electrician.
- When you buy electrical equipment, be sure that it is UL approved.
- Make sure everything has cables that are long enough; never use extension cords.
- Turn off the power before you take equipment out of the pool.
- Have any necessary repairs done by a licensed electrician.
- Never pull an electrical device out of the water by the cable.
- Make sure that the circuit to your pool is protected by a GFI outlet and a fuse or by a GFI circuit breaker.

Note: It is possible today to use low-voltage systems for running many types of pool equipment. This kind of system offers a high degree of protection against accidents. Find out more about low-voltage equipment from dealers selling electrical, aquarium, or garden equipment. These people will also be able to tell you how far solar technology has advanced for use in operating pools.

Drainage

Many pool owners simply let excess water from heavy rains rise and spill over the pool's edge into the garden, where it is absorbed by the soil. This saves you installing a drain, and in many cases it is an adequate solution. But if the soil around the pool cannot absorb the water quickly enough, the area around the pool will stay wet too long or the water will run off into the neighbor's garden, and you may have to dig a drainage pit. This pit carries the water to deeper soil levels before the pool can overflow its banks. You will need a wire compost bin (available at garden centers), some flexible liner, and as many fist-sized rocks as will fit into the bin (for building a drainage pit, see HOW-TO page 53).

As a rule a simple drainage pit as described suffices. If you still have problems with the pool overflowing, you may have to install a regular drain connected to the drainage system of the house. But in such a case you should consult a professional plumber.

Important: Make sure the water does not drain onto a neighbor's property. You are liable for damage resulting from improper disposal of pool water or from defective plumbing.

Technical Equipment for a Garden Pool

In a small pool, proper living conditions for the creatures and plants in it can be obtained only with the help of technical equipment like filters and air and water pumps. If you relied solely on nature, animals and plants would soon perish. For larger pools, where goldfish, kois, or ducks live, technical devices are useful, too, and often indispensable.

There are two things you must always watch out for:

1. The pool water must have plenty of oxygen. Moving water, air pumps, and oxygenating plants will provide oxygen.

2. The pool must never accumulate too much decaying organic matter. Efficient filtering is therefore important. You can buy special pool filters or set up a stream. A stream is the most natural way to filter and aerate the water.

A bird bath should be provided near any pool. Start with a shallow depression in the ground (about 8 square inches or 50 cm^2), put some liner down, and add stones, leaving a small open area in the middle, large enough for the birds to bathe in.

The bird bath should be in an undisturbed spot but where it can be easily observed from some distance. Make sure there are not many bushes close by where cats could hide, ready to pounce on the birds. You will find that there is lots of activity near such a little pool, especially in the early morning hours and in late afternoon.

The Water Pump: A water pump is essential for emptying the pool and changing the water and for moving water over waterfalls and through fountains. It is also useful for circulating water within a pool thus helping to aerate it.

There are a vast number of different pumps, and a buyer without technical know-how will have to rely on advice from knowledgeable sales personnel at a garden center or aquarium store when buying a pump.

Be aware that it has to say specifically on the pump that it is suitable for use in water. It also has to be UL approved. Generally, a water pump should be checked and cleaned once a year (take it to the manufacturer's service center or to the store where you bought it). Find out when you purchase the pump how often it should be brought in for maintenance (once a year is advisable).

Equipment that runs on electricity has to be installed by a licensed electrician. An electric cable mounted improperly in the water can prove deadly to anyone working in the pool.

The Air Pump: Usually a diaphragm air pump is used; it is very useful both in summer and winter for aerating the water. Attach an air stone to the end of the air hose that is in the water. You can get different types of air stones at aquarium stores or garden supply centers.

Important to Know: Normal air pumps should be hung only in a dry place, preferably inside the house. Run the air hose to the pool through a PVC pipe. Pumps with splash-proof housings and so-called garden-pool aerators can be set up outdoors.

Purchase your pump from a store with well-qualified help and inquire how the air pump should be used and maintained.

The Filter: You can buy special garden-pool filters that include circulating pumps. These filters are easy to run and use up very little electricity. All that is required in the line of maintenance is an occasional cleaning or changing of the filter material.

Devices Required for Overwintering: Where winter temperature may remain below freezing, it is often necessary to create an ice-free area in the pond. Practical devices available for this purpose include deicers, which can be constructed of styrofoam (with or without an air pump), and so-called pool heaters (see HOW-TO page 136).

Important: Please consult the section Preventing Accidents Caused by Electricity (page 56).

Safety Precautions for Children

Neither admonishments nor the most patient explanations are very effective at teaching young children that a garden pool is not the same thing as a play basin. Water, especially if there are fish swimming in it, acts like a magnet on children. A shallow shore with a gentle gradient is no guarantee of safety. Access to the pool should be blocked all around the pool and certainly along the steep side of the pool.

Fences

Dry Border Area (lawn, flower beds): A wooden fence 24 inches (60 cm) high with vertical slats whose edges are rounded at the top is appropriate for lawn or flower bed borders. Do not use picket fencing. Children can get hurt on the pointed pickets or stick their heads between them and then be unable to get back out.

If you plant mint, lemon balm, sweet peas, or ivy along the fence, the bare wood will soon be hidden by attractive greenery.

An Important Point: When you buy fencing, be sure to check with the salesperson that the wood is not impregnated with toxic chemicals. These are leached out by rain and may end up in the pool. If you impregnate the wood yourself, do not use any carbolines.

The Marshy Zone: A plastic-coated wiremesh fence is the simplest solution for the marshy area. Choose a 4-inch (10 cm) mesh that allows birds to flit through the holes. A small-mesh fence along a pool can turn into a deadly trap for birds.

When setting up the posts, place angle irons into large flower pots and pour cement footings around them. Then dig the flower pots into the ground. Setting the posts into concrete footings is the most time-consuming part of installing this kind of fencing. The galvanized, plastic-covered mesh is secured to the posts by means of stainless-steel clasps. A simple stretching device gives the fence the necessary tautness.

If you plant some fast-growing reeds along the fence, it will soon be hidden from view.

Flowering rush *(Butomus umbellatus)* always has to be planted in water. Because its roots grow so vigorously, this plant should be set out in containers.

A Safety Grate in the Pool

The grate is placed in the pool horizontally about 4 inches (10 cm) below the water's surface. Use welded, plastic-coated, or galvanized construction steel grating with a mesh size of 2 to 4 inches (6–10 cm). (See drawing, HOW-TO page 53.)

In a pool with a flexible liner, the grate is placed on fired bricks (use perforated red or yellow bricks; do not use cinder block or any masonry products containing lime). In preformed shells that have built-in plant shelves, place the grate on the uppermost shelf. The grate is practically invisible, and water lilies will even grow through it.

Important: Please consult the section on liability at the end of this chapter (see page 61).

Safety Precautions for Animals

It happens not infrequently that mammals (squirrels, mice, household pets) fall into garden pools. Steep banks and smooth surfaces like those of pool liners and fiberglass shells are dangerous traps for them because their feet cannot grab hold of them. You can help these unfortunate accident victims get out by supplying a board. To keep the board from sliding into the pool, it has to be secured in place at the pool's edge. This can be done, for instance, with a piece of liner that is attached to the pool's edge and to the board and acts as a hinge. The extra piece of liner can be glued to the pool's edge or buried in the ground along with the pool liner (see drawing on HOW-TO page 63).

Or you can put a bath mat made of rice straw on the bank with one end hanging deep into the water and the other buried in the bank. The part that is in the water has to be weighted with rocks. If you plant creeping Jenny on both sides of the mat, the plants will spread and practically hide it from view after a while.

Liability in Case of Accidents

Finally, to conclude our discussion of the rather important subject of safety around a pool, we must at least mention the question of liability in case of accidents, a topic that is probably not foremost in the mind of a proud and euphoric new pool owner. We do not have space here for a detailed discussion of the legal situation. But we do want to draw attention to the issue of public safety. You should be aware that you are not only responsible for the safety of your own children but also must, in certain situations, take measures to ensure the safety of other children as well as of adults.

There is a general obligation to provide safe passage across one's property, especially for children. This means that land owners or tenants—if they are aware that children often play on their land and might be exposed to danger—must take permanent and effective measures to protect them from the consequences of their inexperience and negligence.

The attraction a garden pool exerts on children is enormous. Winter brings an added danger, namely ice, which may break if someone steps on it intentionally or inadvertently. (A tip: Leave a fairly long wooden ladder near any large frozen pool. It may prove useful in case an accident should occur in spite of precautions.) The responsibility of a garden pool owner could be stated as follows: If the pool is located on fenced grounds, the owner does not generally have to worry about the safety of trespassers. If an accident should occur, the owner is not liable. But if the pool is not fenced or if the owner is aware that children habitually enter the grounds and play near the pool in spite of repeated warnings and admonitions, safety measures specifically designed to protect children have to be instituted within reasonable financial bounds.

No matter what the situation, liability insurance is always recommended. The pool should be specifically included in the policy. It is therefore a good idea to ask your insurance company to confirm in writing that the policy covers accidents connected with the pool.

In the picture:
The charm of a waterfall. Here it forms the head of a small stream, with water splashing down gaily over the edge of big natural rocks. The increased air humidity resulting from the water spray creates ideal growing conditions for many plants.

HOW-TO: Sealing the Bottom

A Pool Made of Flexible Liner

Use only materials designated specifically as pool liner to seal your garden pool. The manufacturers of these liners guarantee that the special qualities of the liner material will not deteriorate for many years. Thus they will guarantee, for instance, that the liner is ultraviolet-light resistant, impermeable to roots, tearproof, heat and cold resistant, will not disintegrate, and is free of substances harmful to plants or animals.

Other kinds of plastic, like the ones used in construction to protect foundations against moisture, are totally unsuitable.

Putting Down the Liner

Drawing 1

After the pool cavity has been excavated, you have to remove any sharp-edged objects, such as nails, rocks, or buried construction rubble. Sharp edges of rocks too large to move have to be chipped away until they are more or less rounded and smooth.

To protect the pool liner against damage from below it is advisable to put down a protective pad (available at pet supply stores or garden centers). If the bottom is hard or rocky, cover it first with 2 to 4 inches (5–10 cm) of sand, and lay the pad on top of that.

Position the liner to extend about 12 inches (30 cm) beyond the pool's rim all the way around.

As soon as the liner is in place, start running water slowly into the pool and continue until the pool is three quarters full. The pressure of the water will push the liner flush against the walls. As the water rises, smooth out folds that may form or arrange them so they will not stand out visually later on. There is no need to get rid of all the folds because they do not affect the liner's durability. You can make small corrections in the pool's profile by raising the liner at the pool's edge and adding or removing sand or earth. If major corrections are needed, you will have to pump out some of the water.

Fastening the Liner to the Pool's Edge

Drawing 2

Where the edge of the pool will not be walked on you do not need to reinforce the bank, but it is important to place the liner with the ends sticking out of the soil line. This prevents dry garden soil around the pool from withdrawing water from the pool.

Reinforcing the bank

Drawing 3

In sections of the pool's edge that will be walked on, the bank must be reinforced. Rocks can be used to provide the necessary firmness. To prevent abrasion or puncture damage to the liner, the rocks should be covered with a pad. Then pull the liner over them and bury it in the soil, but make sure that the end points upward. Round logs or square beams also provide good reinforcement.

2. Position the liner so that the ends point upward; this way water will not seep over the edge.

3. Border areas that get a lot of foot traffic must be reinforced. This can be done with rocks, for instance.

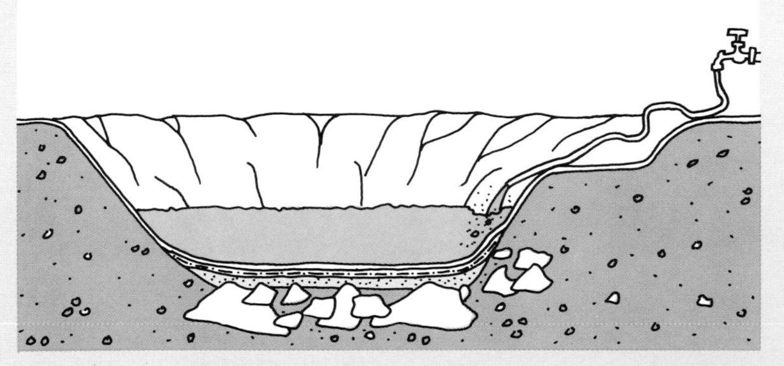

1. Sealing a pool with a liner. Remove all sharp-edged objects from the excavation. If there are rocks at the bottom, put down a layer of sand and lay a protective pad under the liner.

If you want to have flagstones along the pool's edge, be sure to place a protective pad between them and the pool liner, or add about 2 inches (5 cm) of sand on top of the liner to protect it.

Using a Preformed Shell

Preformed pool shells come in many shapes and sizes. You can get anything from rectangular pools to round, oval, L-shaped, and kidney-shaped ones. The sizes of prefabricated pools range from 250 gallons (1,000 l) to setups composed of

4. Place a preformed shell in the spot intended for it, and mark its outline on the ground with the help of a plumb line and a carpenter's level. Trace a second line 20 inches (50 cm) farther out all the way around because you will need extra space to backfill around the shell.

several pool elements that can be combined and hold several times as much.

Reputable manufacturers guarantee that the materials the shells are made of are safe for plants and animals as well as resistant to ultraviolet light, decay, freezing, and physical impact.

Marking the Outline
Drawing 4
If the manufacturer does not supply a special pattern of the pool's shape for tracing the outline, you will have to use a large square or plumb lines. Add a rim of about 20 inches (50 cm) all around to give you enough room later on for backfilling.

Installing the Shell
Drawing 5
Start digging where the deepest point of the pool will be. Make sure the excavation is about 6 inches (15 cm) wider and 2 to 4 inches (5–10 cm) deeper than the shell everywhere, including any bulges. Then pour 2 to 4 inches (5–10 cm) of damp sand in the deepest area. Smooth the sand and tamp it solid with a mason's trowel. Now lower the shell in place and check that the top is level. Immediately start water running into the shell, but do so slowly and backfill all around the outside of the shell with sand and water, making sure all hollow pockets get filled in. You must work patiently so that later on the shell will not settle deeper or tilt to one side. Backfilling is done as follows: Fill the space around the deepest point of the shell with sand and tamp it solid with a board. To wash grains of sand into air spaces that may remain, run some water slowly onto the sand. Go on from one area to the next doing this, slowly filling each with sand and water alternately, and work your way upward step by step.

Pool Margin that Will Not Be Walked On
Drawing 6
Here all you need to do is put down pieces of sod that may be left over from excavating the pool cavity. The sod can run all the way down to the water's edge, or you may prefer to plant the pool margin with ground covers, special grasses, or ornamental shrubs.

Pool Margin that Will Be Walked On
Drawing 7
Rocks can be used to reinforce the bank in these areas. Pile them as you would for a loose-rock wall, and fill the spaces between them with earth or sand. Cover with fieldstones, flagstones or concrete slabs.

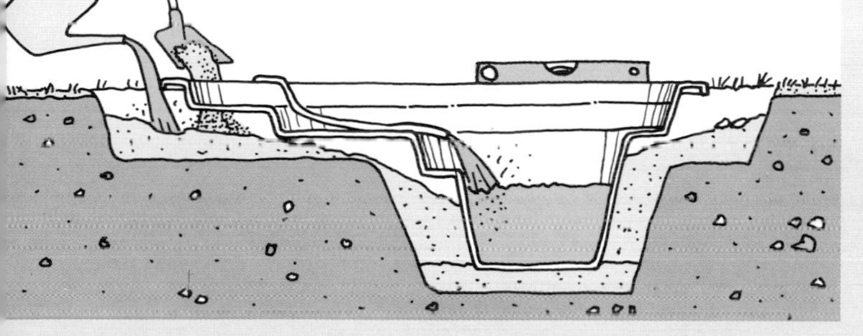

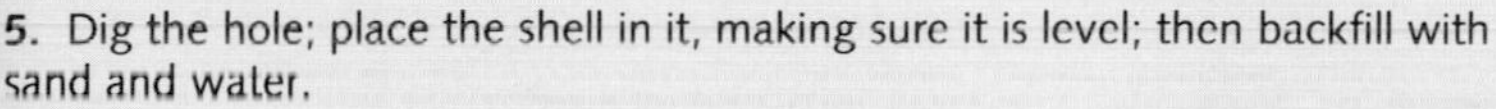

5. Dig the hole; place the shell in it, making sure it is level; then backfill with sand and water.

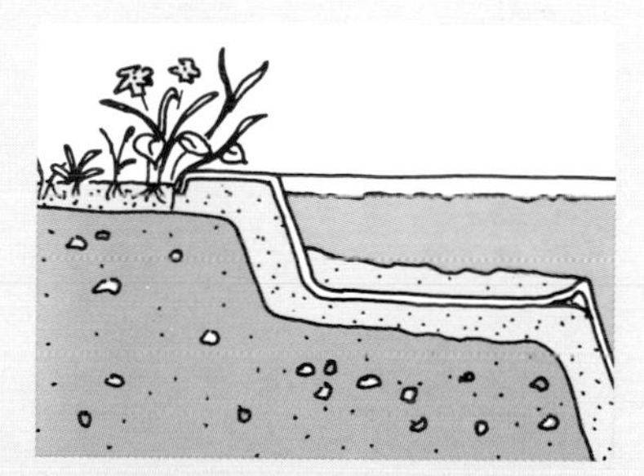

6. Where the edge will not be walked on, no special reinforcement of the bank is needed.

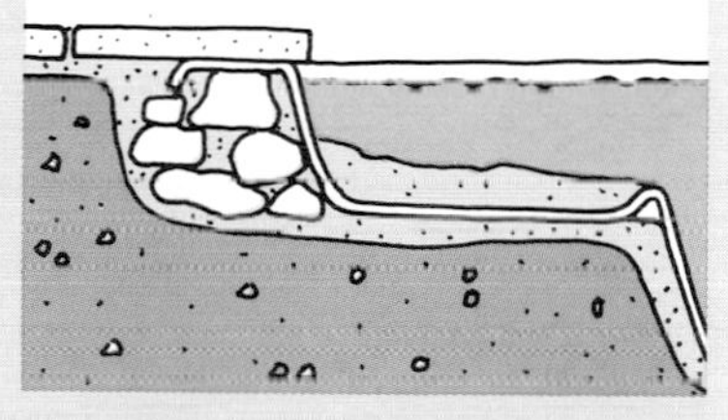

7. In places where there will be foot traffic, reinforce the bank with rocks.

A stream bed leading from pool to pool. The water is dammed at different levels by wooden beams and meanders through the garden in wide bends. The profusion of thriving plants and the lovely flowering day lilies in the foreground show that this is the work of an expert.

A Stream in the Garden

What nature lover does not feel soothed and refreshed by the cheerful rushing of a mountain stream or the soft babbling of a meadow brook. These sounds are indeed music to our ears. Following along a stream on a mountain hike or on a stroll in the countryside, especially if the stream is unspoiled and abounding with wild plants and animal life, we experience the kind of happiness that is so beautifully expressed by one of the songs in Schubert's cycle "The Fair Maiden of the Mill," where the young wanderer sings:

I heard a little brook rippling
From a mountain spring,
Rushing down to the valley,
So clear and sparkling.

Streams and brooks were much celebrated by the Romantic poets. Nature first entered music and literature as a major theme at that time, and moving water came to symbolize for poets and composers both constancy and the longing for the faraway. In today's life, when nature is forced into the background more and more, we should not hesitate to introduce it into our immediate environment whenever we can. A running stream allows us more than anything else to experience first-hand a very special "piece of nature" in our own backyard.

But today finding such walks is not all that easy. Streams have fared no better than other natural bodies of water—ponds, lakes, ditches, and swales. They have been straightened out, covered over with pavement, misused as dumping grounds, or they have simply disappeared.

Why not recreate some of the much sung beauty and romance of a stream in your backyard by setting up a stream bed there? For even in a garden, a stream offers fascinating possibilities for planting, acts as a biological filter, and, more important, provides a place to live for many creatures. Practical tips can be found on the following pages.

Streams in Nature

In nature no stream is quite like any other. Natural streams—if they have not been degraded into artificial, straight channels—are as varied as the landscapes they traverse.

Even a single stream exhibits variety as it runs from its source to its destination. Each section of its course presents a different aspect, displaying its own characteristic plant and animal populations.

All streams have three features in common: water that flows downward; a source, which marks the upper end of the stream's surface course; and a lower end or mouth. A stream can flow into another stream or river or into a body of flat, or lentic, water. Or it may disappear from view, make its way underground for a while, and either reappear again farther downstream or drain into the ground water.

We can divide streams roughly into two types:

Mountain Streams: These are characterized by a strong gradient and a rocky bottom, with the result that the water rushes down at a great speed. It is possible to distinguish several subtypes, such as alpine streams, hill country streams, and glacial streams.

Meadow Brooks: Typically, meadow brooks have a low gradient and a sandy to pebbly bottom. What is often striking about them is their curving course. Since at a low gradient water moves slowly, obstacles cause bends and detours in the stream's course; the stream, we say, meanders. Some of these obstacles are created by the stream itself. After heavy rains or when the snow melts in the spring, water volume and speed of flow can increase dramatically, and the stream may carry along objects like downed trees for a distance, later depositing them in its own path, and then a new way has to be found around them.

There are no general rules about the length and width of streams. The length is often hard to determine because streams may run underground for a stretch now and then. The width can be anything from a narrow rill to a few feet or much more. It is hard to say at what width a stream is more properly called a river. Experts use the volume of flow to help decide whether a body of moving water is a large stream or a small river.

You can construct a small waterfall quite inexpensively from ready-made parts. You can buy waterfall basins made of sandstone (as in this picture), ceramic, or fiberglass.

Ecological Reasons for Creating a Stream in Your Garden

Quite apart from the fact that anyone who loves wild rivers will be eager to create his or her own version of an ideal stream if at all possible, there is much to be said for having a stream in the garden.

A Stream as Complement or Alternative to a Garden Pool

Garden pools are becoming quite common these days as more and more people realize how beautiful water looks in a garden. However, many gardeners cannot quite see the point or the usefulness of a stream. The lack of enthusiasm is due, most of all, to the fact that people imagine setting up a stream must be very difficult and that they don't realize how effective a stream is at bringing "a piece of nature" into the garden.

A Stream as a Biological Filter: If you already have a garden pool, a properly laid out stream can effectively take over the function of a filter. What you have to do in that case is to install a water pump that will feed the pool water into the stream, which will then return it again to the pool. The pool water is thus circulated continuously through the stream bed, depositing products of organic decomposition there. These are broken down by bacteria living in the stream and transformed into nutrients that become directly available to the plants. This way the stream, acting as a biological filter, keeps the water clear and helps maintain the biological balance in the pool, while simultaneously adding oxygen to the pool water. That is why it is highly recommended that all pools, but especially those that contain fish, be connected to a stream.

The Microclimate Along the Stream: A favorable microclimate develops along a stream, furthering plant growth. Many plants that grow profusely along the banks would barely be able to hold their own if there were no stream in your garden.

Running a stream alongside of or through a vegetable garden can create a favorable microclimate that will encourage more luxuriant growth of the vegetables. But be careful! Make sure no fertilizer

Types of streams in nature.
Above: A meadow stream, still in its wild state, making its way down a gentle slope by way of several distinct steps.
Below: In flat terrain a meadow stream carves its course through the countryside in meandering curves.

is carried into the stream by the rain; otherwise you will have exces sive amounts of nutrients in your pool, which will lead to alga problems.

A stream also adds beauty to a rock garden.

A Stream Without a Garden Pool: A stream also functions ver well without a garden pool. It can be designed and planted t appear just as varied as a stream that is connected to a pool (se drawing, HOW-TO page 75).

A garden stream is safe for children because the water in it is s shallow. Anyone who is reluctant to install a garden pool becaus there are small children around but who still would like to hear th sound of water in the garden can set up a stream and add a poc later, when the children are older. In that case you would, of course have to think ahead and reserve space for the pool when you pla your stream.

Stream Models: A stream cannot be compared to a garden pool which is conceived with a definite purpose in mind (see pool mod els, such as A Natural Pond on page 18 or A Koi Pool on page 29) Instead, as already said, the very nature of a stream is that it i made up of different segments. It is only for these individual seg ments—the source, a waterfall, a small dam, a marshy zone, an the end of the course—that we can make any design suggestion (see drawing, HOW-TO page 75).

The two types of natural streams we have described, namely th mountain stream and the meadow brook, can serve as genera models. As a rule, a stream running through the garden shoul resemble a babbling meadow brook; that is, it should flow gentl and slowly.

If you were to set up a 20-foot (6 m) stream like a mountai stream for its full length, the result would be quite boring. In addi tion, the stream would attract hardly any plants or animals becaus many of them don't like rushing water. But you might very we want to arrange one section as a mountain stream (see drawing HOW-TO page 75), routing it through a rock garden, for instance There it would fit naturally into the "landscape."

Practical Tips for Setting Up a Stream Bed

The great variability of natural streams cannot be duplicated in a garden stream, but is a useful ideal to keep in mind. The more it i part of our conception, the more attractive and interesting th stream will turn out to be. We are not talking here about copyin nature, which we could not do if we tried, but about being awar of the many different features that make up a stream. One thing t strive for, for example, is to construct the stream bed and bank differently in the different sections. Widenings and bends, marshy strip several feet wide alongside the stream, a series o small dams, rocks and pebbles in the stream bed, and varyin water levels all enliven the water and affect its speed. In bays an behind rocks and roots the water comes to rest, and it is especiall these quiet pools that are favored by plants and animals that live i and along streams.

An idyllic piedmont scene. The meadow through which the brook wends its way still has many wildflowers, including the marsh marigold (which also does well in gardens along a stream), and cuckoo flower.

Planning the Stream's Course

Paper and pencil and a long garden hose or rope are just as essential in the planning of a stream as they are for designing a pool.

The Stream's Length: If the stream is to double as a biological filter the rule of thumb is to figure on 5 feet (1.5 m) of stream per 250 gallons (1,000 L) of pool water. To give an example: Since a pool of 60 square feet (6 m^2) holds about 1,000 gallons (4,000 L), a stream connected to it should be about 20 feet (6 m) long.

Length is of less importance in a stream that is not connected to a pool. But it should not be too short, or the water will not flow properly. Figure on a minimum of at least 15 feet (5 m).

The Stream's Course: Your stream will most likely end up longer than the minimum given here. This is because once you start marking the stream's course you will find that even a small garden will accommodate quite a long stream. Run it along the fence, incorpo-

Stream beds in the garden. These two small waterfalls are at the head of their respective streams and are flanked by planted ferns. Garden flowers also thrive here, as does moss, which covers the rocks with its rich green.

rate some S-curves around trees, or have it meander in wide oxbows across the lawn. Experiment with the garden hose, a long rope, or both. You will be amazed at how many feet you will lay down without it seeming to be too much.

Width and Depth of the Stream Bed: Use your spade as a measuring stick. An ideal average size for a stream bed is 1 spade's length deep (about 10 inches or 25 cm) and 2 spades' lengths wide (about 20 inches or 50 cm). These dimensions will work in any garden. Wider streams are suitable only for large gardens because the curves take up a lot of space. Narrower streams of about 12 inches (30 cm) are still functional, but if they get narrower than that, they become mere rivulets through which the water can be moved only with difficulty. The dimensions indicated are meant merely as guidelines.

Although the water in a garden stream is driven by a pump, its liveliness and the desired leisurely speed are the result of several features:

- Varied water depths—dig the stream bed to different depths or add varying amounts of fill in different spots when you first set up the stream's course.
- Obstacles in the stream bed—add rocks.
- Narrow channels—place rocks or containers with plants in the water along both banks.
- Bulges in the stream bed—arrange small or larger marshy areas (see drawings, HOW-TO page 74) or bays (minipools) at least 3 feet (1 m) wide here and there along the stream bed.

You can plant even the smallest garden stream with a variety of plants. The prominent flower here is the silverdust primrose *(Primula pulverulenta)*.

Things to Keep in Mind When Setting Up the Stream Bed

You do not need heavy earth-moving machinery to dig a stream bed, but do allow plenty of time for the job, for the more carefully you shape the stream bed the better the stream will function and the greater will be your rewards.

In addition to acquainting yourself with the basic principles discussed in the next few paragraphs you should also look at the informative drawings and detailed instructions presented in the HOW-TO pages 74–75.

The Gradient: In most gardens it will be necessary to provide the gradient by artificial means. However, no dramatic difference in elevation is required between the source and the end of the stream since you are building a stream, not a waterfall.

The numbers that follow can serve as a basic guideline: A gradient of 1 to 2 percent (about 1/8–1/4 inch per foot or 1–2 cm per 1 m of length) is sufficient; in other words, a difference in height of about a foot and a half (50 cm) between the top and the bottom of a stream about 20 feet (6 m) long is sufficient.

Supplying the Gradient: Simply piling up earth will not result in a solid base for a stream bed. Instead, the gradient should be supplied by building terracelike steps into the stream bed. These steps, which may be quite wide and of different height have to be supported with laths, round or square logs, or rocks.

The gradient should not be the same throughout the stream's course. A good pattern to follow is to have several drops at the beginning (a waterfall, an overflowing basin, a succession of small dams) and then to let the stream meander lazily along a shallow course as it approaches the inlet to the pool (see drawing, HOW-TO page 75).

Materials to Hold the Water: Flexible pool liner, preformed shells, and so-called stream basins made either of fiberglass or of natural rock are used. You can also combine basins and pool liner.

If you have to glue several lengths of liner together, be sure to observe the directions that come with the adhesive (adhesive materials are available at aquarium supply stores and garden centers).

Fill: A stream bed with a liner should always be filled with gravel and larger stones, and some stones should also be added to the stream basins. You can use the various kinds of fill including fine gravel (diameter $^{3}/_{16}$–$^{1}/_{4}$ inch or 5–7 mm) and quartz gravel (available at aquarium stores and building supply or garden centers). Do not use any limestone gravel because it may make the water too alkaline. You need about 50 pounds (25 kg) of fill per yard of stream bed.

Reinforcing the Banks: It is especially important to reinforce the places that are built up to provide gradient and the banks along bends because the current tends to wash away the soil there. Rocks, coarse river gravel, and round logs work well.

A Water Pump: Pumps with a capacity of 100 gallons (6 watt) to 500 gallons (19 watt) (250 and 1,000 L, respectively) are quite sufficient. Low-voltage pumps can also be used for propelling the water.

Pumps with a higher capacity (such as the ones used to run big water fountains) should not be used. They make the stream run

This artificially constructed stream looks remarkably like a wild stream. The water is making its way between natural rocks of various sizes.

too fast, since the speed of flow is determined not only by the gradient and shape of the stream bed but also by the volume of water.

A garden stream should flow slowly because a fast-flowing stream cannot develop the filtering action that is so beneficial for a garden pool. A fast-flowing stream is not desirable even if you have no pool, for most plants and animals do not like fast-moving water. A stream traversing a rock garden represents a special case; here more powerful pumps are needed.

The Source: The water for the stream comes either from the garden pool, or, if there is no pool, it can emerge from a bubbler stone or a water spout that is connected to the pump by a garden hose.

The End of the Stream: The stream can terminate by flowing into the garden pool, preferably by way of a small waterfall, which will supply an extra dose of oxygen for the pool. If there is no pool, the water can flow into a catch basin with a pump that will move the water back up to the source by way of an attached garden hose. Instead of a simple water pump you may use a pool biofilter with a built-in pump (for pump capacity, see above). The fact is that because of the constant motion of the water, dust particles keep being carried along. Plain water pumps are equipped with a filter, but they tend to clog up quickly, and then the gallon capacity drops rapidly. The result is that less and less water flows down the stream bed. That is why I recommend the use of a pool biofilter, which largely prevents buildup. A good filler material for such a filter is tiny ceramic tubes (available at aquarium stores).

Upkeep: During the summer, the stream should run continually day and night. No special maintenance is needed during that time. In the fall the stream is turned off, the pump taken out of the pool or the catch basin, the plants cut back or thinned, and the fish moved to an aquarium or pool where they are safe for the winter.

In the spring the fill has to be rinsed with a sharp spray of water. Then, when the pump is turned on again, the stream will resume its cheerful burbling for many months. If the stream is connected to a pool, a third of the pool water should be changed after spring cleaning to get rid of the dirty stream water.

Above: Cotton grass *(Eriophorum)* grows as high as 24 inches (60 cm), depending on the species. It does not grow in water and should be planted in soil that is a mixture of sand, clay, and peat.
Below: Floating pondweed *(Potamogeton natans)* competes with algae for food. Since it multiplies rapidly, it has to be thinned regularly.

Plants for the Stream

The stream bed and the banks offer lots of room for all kinds of attractive plants. Plants can be set directly into the ground along the dry, damp, or boggy bank. Plants to be set in the stream itself are placed into long, narrow containers.

To plant the dry and damp banks of the stream and the marshy areas you may have set up, you can choose from among all the plants listed later under various soil and moisture conditions for use in and around garden pools (plant survey on HOW-TO pages 108–109). But for the stream bed itself your choice is restricted to plants that flourish naturally in moving water. Among these are wild calla *(Calla palustris)* with its attractive white spathe (caution: the calla's red berries are poisonous); marsh marigold *(Caltha palustris)*, which flowers profusely; creeping Jenny *(Lysimachia nummularia)*; the undemanding arrowhead *(Sagittaria latifolia)*, which is an efficient oxygenator and competes for food with algae; and brooklime *(Veronica beccabunga)*, which forms decorative, bright blue cushions.

HOW-TO: Setting Up a Stream

Sealing the Stream Bed and Reinforcing the Bank

Once you have prepared the stream bed and provided the appropriate gradient (see page 71), you have to seal the bottom. Pool liner is the best material to use. First figure out how much you need. To measure the width, lay a garden hose across the bed, then measure the amount of hose used and add 12 inches (30 cm) on each side, that is, a total of 24 inches (60 cm), for holding the ends in place. Then measure the desired length of the stream with the aid of the hose. You should add a good 3 feet (1 m) to the length.

1. Seal the stream bed with pool liner. Fine and coarse gravel works well as fill for the stream bed.

2. A marshy zone along the stream provides an additional habitat for plants and wildlife.

Most suppliers of pool liner will cut and glue together the strips of liner for you for a small charge. If you want to glue the strips yourself, be sure to ask how the particular adhesive you buy is used and follow the instructions carefully. The substances contained in these glues are harmful to your health if not handled properly.

Reinforcing the Banks, Positioning the Liner, and Adding Fill

Drawing 1

Before laying down the liner you should reinforce the banks with rocks or with posts dug vertically into the ground. Reinforcement is especially important where the stream bed has been built up to provide the necessary gradient and along bends because soil erosion is more likely to occur. After these preparations, position the liner in the stream bed and add the fill. You will need approximately 50 pounds (25 kg) of fill per yard of stream bed. Fill the stream bed up enough so that the tops of the plant containers to be placed in the stream will be hidden by the gravel.

Give the stream a trial run before you attach the liner to the bank. Pump some water into the stream bed and watch how fast it flows down. The stream should run slowly. You can reduce the speed by widening the stream bed; deepening it will speed up the flow.

The final step is to pull the liner over the bank and bury it under the soil with the edge pointing upward. Now all that is left to do is to put the containers with aquatic plants in the stream and place some fist-sized stones in the stream bed.

Creating a Small Marshy Area

Drawing 2

Widen the stream bed in a few places and place stones around these wider pockets. This results in a small marsh, through which the water moves slowly and which therefore becomes a refuge for amphibians and various other animals. Add earth to these wet areas and plant marsh plants.

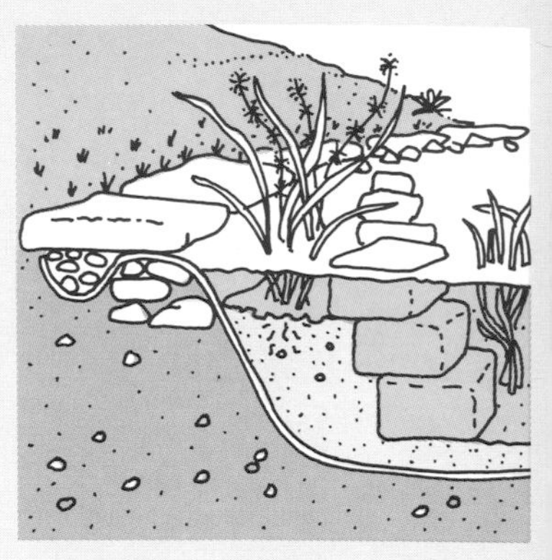

3. Flagstones along the bank look very attractive. If there will be foot traffic along the stream, you will have to provide a solid base by placing a layer of rocks underneath the flagstones.

Lining the Bank with Flagstones

Drawing 3

You can put down flagstones in places along the stream that will be walked on frequently. To keep the flagstones from sinking into the ground you will have to build a support of rocks or logs. Place some padding between the liner and the flagstones to prevent abrasion.

Model of a Stream Without a Pool

Drawing 4

The stream starts at the highest point of elevation, forms a waterfall, is then guided along an S-shaped course, and ends in a marsh bed about 1 foot (30 cm) deep, out of which the water flows into a collection pit. In this pit, which should be about 28 inches (70 cm) deep and covered with metal grating, there is a pump that moves the water out through a garden hose and up again to the head of the stream.

To replenish the water supply, that is, to replace water lost through evaporation, you will want to run another garden hose from the water faucet to the stream. This hose may be connected to a water fountain.

The first section of the stream bed has a greater gradient than the lower ones and is built the same way as the large, widespread waterfall described in detail in HOW-TO pages 92–93. After the waterfall, the stream bed should wend its way, becoming flatter and flatter, toward the point of termination—in this model, a small marsh. But the stream could just as well empty into a garden pool.

Recreating a Mountain Stream
Drawing 5
To set up the entire stream like a mountain brook makes little sense since the water would run much too fast and the stream would provide no filtering action. But for a short stretch, preferably right after a waterfall, a section of mountain stream can be a charming variation. Setting it up is quite simple: All you need to do is to line the stream bed with large rocks. The rocks don't block the water but offer just enough resistance to make it rush and tumble around them, the way it does in a real mountain stream.

Sealing the Bed with Clay
If you use clay to seal the bottom of your stream, you can reinforce the banks with woven willow twigs. This method has a long history. It has been traditionally used in the past to keep streams from changing their course and flowing too close to settlements.

Reinforcing the Banks with Willow Fences
Drawing 6
Weave willow branches together to form a "fence" that is slightly higher than the stream bed. Then run the fence along the sides of the stream bed, sticking it into the clay while it is still wet. Fill in the space outside the fence with twigs and clay. The willow branches will produce shoots within the first year and will eventually grow into shrubs and trees. For the vertical posts you can use birch, alder, goat willow, or poplar; the branches running horizontally should come from goat or osier willows. To keep the banks in shape you have to keep cutting away anything that grows toward the water. If you trim on the other side, the trees or bushes will become lopsided on the stream side and eventually topple into the water.

4. An example of a stream without a pool. The stream terminates in a large marshy area connected to a collection pit. The water is returned to the head of the stream or "spring" by means of a pump and attached garden hose.

5. A section of the stream can be designed to imitate a mountain stream. This stream section should come right after a waterfall.

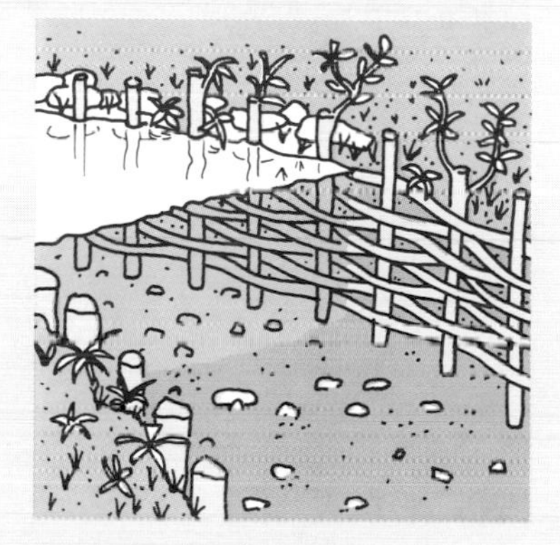

6. The banks of a stream with a clay bed can be reinforced with willow branches that are woven together.

Design Ideas for the Surroundings

You have finished building your pool, and now it is time to think about how you want its border to look and which portions of it need to be reinforced so that they can be walked on. A good way to begin is to survey all the various possibilities and to determine which materials and design elements would fit well with the basic concept of your pool and with your garden as a whole. After all, you want to end up with something that has some artistic unity. Don't forget foot bridges, docks, and islands; these elements are not only practical but can also lend a special elegance to a pool.

The Pool's Edge—To Be Walked On or Not?

A pool where you can walk around on all sides can be just as attractive as one that is bordered all the way around with plants. There is a third alternative that has proven both practical and attractive, namely, a compromise between the two. If some of the border can be walked on, this allows you to observe the life in the pool from up close, and feeding the fish as well as maintenance chores are made easy. At the same time, the parts of the pool margin that are not open to traffic remain undisturbed and can serve as a habitat for plants and wildlfe.

Planning Borders that Will Be Walked On: You will get many ideas for designing a sturdy border by looking over the photos in this book. In addition, some attractive, tried-and-true methods are presented in HOW-TO pages 82–83, complete with explanations and illustrations.

Along the Untrodden Parts of the Shore: For the undisturbed edge, materials to work with are plants and rocks. Different kinds of borders, like a small marshy area, a planted bank, or a rocky edge or a rock wall, are also depicted in a number of the photos. Drawings showing how to proceed are found on HOW-TO page 63.

A pool adjacent to a house offers many intriguing design possibilities—such as this wooden dock leading from the terrace across the water.

In the picture:
The tall purple loosestrife and the fountain grass seem to practically grow into the living room.

Materials for the Pool Margin

The more natural the material, the more beautiful it is. This is the motto you should follow when choosing your materials. Wood and stone are natural materials. One "approved" exception to this rule are concrete blocks, which nowadays no longer look as dreary as did the uniform gray slabs used in earlier times. In the following sections you will find practical tips for buying and using materials. Examples of design ideas, complete with instructions and drawings are on HOW-TO pages 82–83.

Stone

What is meant here is natural, unfinished stone, which is just as versatile and decorative around a pool as wood. Especially useful are pebbles and cobbles, that is, stones worn round and smooth in rivers. They come in all sizes, from a fraction of an inch in diameter to fist size. Larger stones, small boulders, and ashlar also look attractive, either hewn or left in their natural state.

Any metamorphic or igneous rocks can be used if they don't give off chemical substances that can contaminate the water. Among recommended rocks are pebbles; red, green, and black slate; sandstone; lava; and basalt.

Not recommended is limestone because rain continually leaches water hardeners out of it.

Japanese iris *(Iris ensata)*. Many gorgeously colored varieties of this old Japanese garden flower are now readily available. The Japanese iris likes sun and moist ground. Depending on the variety, it flowers from mid-June to late July.

Uses for Stone: Pebbles and other natural stone can be used both to provide a firm base for the bank and as a visible element in the design of a pool's edge. One simple yet very decorative solution is to build a stone wall: Pile the rocks on top of each other, attaching the lighter ones with silicone glue to keep them from sliding out of place.

Using split rocks or ashlar, it is not difficult to build a loose-rock wall that could support a steep bank, for instance, or the downhill side of a pool (see drawing, HOW-TO page 47). If the rocks are relatively flat they can also be laid along the pool's edge, like concrete blocks.

Some Useful Suggestions: You can buy cobbles and pebbles at building supply centers just about anywhere, but other natural stone is sometimes hard to find. In some areas there are firms that sell special rock varieties (check the yellow pages in your phone book). In many rural areas it is worth asking farmers if they would like to get rid of stones and rocks that have accumulated in the course of clearing and working the fields.

Note: The perforated bricks repeatedly mentioned in this book are extremely useful as well as cheap. These unglamorous bricks that one sees at any construction site have become a valuable aid for all kinds of projects. Especially in pool building they can be put to many uses; they can be piled up to separate the marshy area off from the swimming pool or serve as a platform for water-lily baskets or for stepping stones. Make sure you place them with the holes pointing sideways, so that the water can flow through them horizontally. You can buy these bricks at any building supply center.

Pavement

Small paved areas in the garden near the pool look especially nice because the small stones—whether carefully arranged in decorative patterns or placed in seemingly random fashion—harmonize with the materials used around the pool's margin. A combination of pavers and square timbers (don't use railroad ties, which are preserved with creosote or petroleum distillates) or larger stones looks very attractive. These days many choices are available. There are pavers of natural stone, concrete, and of red brick, as well as of wood. It is true that the careful laying of the pavers in a bed of sand is time consuming; on the other hand, the resulting surface will remain water-absorbent forever and is—at least if stone is used—practically indestructible.

A pavement made of pressure-treated wood, usually in the form of slices taken from tree trunks, is also very long lasting.

The photo on pages 24–25—which may serve as inspiration for creating a similar scene—shows a lovely paved area near the pool that invites the visitor to stop and sit and relax. On HOW-TO page 83 you will find instructions on how to build a pavement of wood. Stone or concrete pavers are laid similarly.

Flagstones

Included here are not only natural flagstones but also blocks of concrete or aggregate that are used for paths and patios.

Natural flagstones are frost-resistant, but they are expensive and not all that easy to work with. You must work very carefully and slowly to place these irregularly shaped flat rocks correctly.

Concrete blocks of a quality suitable to the purpose can look just as good as flagstones, and they can be considered an economical solution only in comparison to the price of natural flagstones. Their surfaces do not have the drab, gray look we usually associate with concrete. Apart from the paths constructed with modest gray squares and the old familiar ones made with pebbles or gravel pressed into the surface, you can now buy so-called decorator blocks for pathways and patios. These come in the most varied textures and colors. However, not all of them look right near a pool. Many of the designs and colors are more suited to the context of an elegant patio with trimmed shrubs growing in tubs than to a pool surrounded by natural vegetation. The larger the area you are going to cover with concrete blocks, the plainer they should be.

A bubbler stone basin in an atrium garden. The irregular stones of different sizes make a nice contrast to the geometrically arranged granite squares of the pavement.

Above: A roofed pool in front of the living room. The strip of cobbles along the outer edge combines with the wood of the rafters and with the water to form a harmonious whole.
Below: A miniature pool set-up for limited space. Because of the interestingly varied arrangement of steps, water levels, and other surfaces—some of wood, others paved with stones—the space between the house and the fence is made to appear larger than it really is.

Uses for Flagstones: Lay flagstones along the side of the pool where you want to make a walkway. Examples are shown in the photos on pages 39 and 40–41. Drawings showing how to lay the stones can be found on HOW-TO pages 82–83.

Support for the Flagstones: Flagstones have to rest on a solid base. The steeper the pool's side, the more support has to be provided. If the bank is quite steep, a wall of perforated bricks or of medium-sized rocks should be built as support. Where the shore is flat, some large stones are all that is needed.

Important: Do not use stones or concrete blocks with smooth or polished surfaces. Such a surface turns extremely slippery if it gets wet, turning the pool's edge into a treacherous slide and a potential source of accidents.

Wood

It is hard to imagine what we would do if wood were eliminated as a material for use in landscape design. Wood fits harmoniously into a garden because, as a natural material, it never looks out of place there and lends—even in large structures like pergolas, pavilions, and arbors—an aura of natural warmth. The photos on pages 23, 80, and 127 show just how attractive wood can look near a pool.

Uses of Wood: Wood can be used for reinforcing the bank, for the pool's border, for building bridges and docks, and for the construction of waterfalls. (In the latter instance wood serves primarily as supporting timbers.) Round and square logs look attractive and are versatile. Sunk partially into the ground, whether in the shape of vertical posts or of horizontal beams, they fulfill two functions at the same time: The part that is buried acts as reinforcement for the bank while the part that sticks up above the ground forms a visually pleasing pool border that can be walked on (for examples, see drawings, HOW-TO pages 82, 83, and 93).

Some Useful Suggestions: Many building supply centers and lumber yards sell round posts, square timbers, boards for docks and boardwalks, and many other items in a special section that contains only wood designed specifically for garden use. Generally, this wood has been pressure-treated to resist decay even if the wood is in constant contact with soil. Always ask specifically for pressure-treated wood because wood treated by this method is most suitable for use near pools.

You should always place a layer of pool liner between the wood and the pool water to prevent harmful substances in the wood from entering the water. No matter how wood is used, sealing it off with pool liner never presents a great problem. It never pays to pinch pennies when buying wood for use near a pool. Do not let anyone talk you into buying cheap construction lumber, let alone railroad ties that have been contaminated with herbicides or oil, or both. Regular building lumber rots too fast and thus should never be used to reinforce a bank. Railroad ties contain chemicals that will be washed out by rain or the pool water and may poison your pool or even end up in the ground water.

A simple bridge with rope railings connects the circular wooden terrace to the garden.

HOW-TO: Constructing the Pool's Edge

1. A boardwalk along the pool's edge is supported by a substructure of gravel, sand, cinder blocks, and supporting timbers.

Ideas and Practical Tips for Designing the Edge

The design of the margin is what lends a pool its distinctive air. Wood and stone offer many possibilities for achieving a harmonious transition from the pool to the garden. These HOW-TO pages offer you ideas and instructions for making different kinds of borders and also help you solve the problems presented by a steep bank that is to be used as a walkway.

A Wooden Dock Running Along the Pool's Edge

Drawing 1

Wooden boards arranged as for a bridge do not necessarily have to lead across the pool (see HOW-TO page 92) or jut out over the water to provide a dock for bathers, as shown on page 46. They can equally well run along the pool's edge to provide a boardwalk instead of stepping stones of natural rock or concrete blocks. You can buy suitable wood—boards and supporting timbers—at a lumber yard or a building supply center. You can even have the lumber cut to the desired size there (coat the cut surfaces with a wood preservative). Gravel, sand, and cinder blocks for the footing to rest on can also be purchased there.

This is how you proceed: Dig away the earth along the pool to a depth of about 10 inches (25 cm); the excavation should be long enough and wide enough to accommodate the boardwalk. Put down a layer of gravel about 4 or 6 inches (10–15 cm) deep. Test to see how far apart the supporting timbers should be. For a walkway about 1 yard (1 m) wide, you need three timbers, with the outer ones placed along the outside in such a way that the edges of the boards protrude a couple of inches; the third supporting timber is centered between the other two. Lay the cinder blocks on the gravel for the supporting timbers to rest on. Fill the space between the cinder blocks with sand. Then put the supporting timbers in place and fasten the boards to them with rustproof nails or screws.

If you do not want to build the boardwalk yourself, you can buy ready-made parts and assemble them, but this is more expensive than building from scratch.

Nail the pool liner to the supporting timbers facing the water, and cover the ends with a board.

Finishing the Edge Along a Steep Bank

Drawing 2

If a steep bank of the pool is going to be walked on, it has to be reinforced. The following is one simple method to achieve this: Take so-called edging or curbing stones and set them on edge almost vertically in the earth along the bank. Pull the liner over them and weigh it down behind the edging stones with rocks, but make sure the end of the liner sticks upward. If you purchase pool bank or bank planting mats that include plant pockets you can even plant steep banks. To do this, fill the plant pockets with soil and

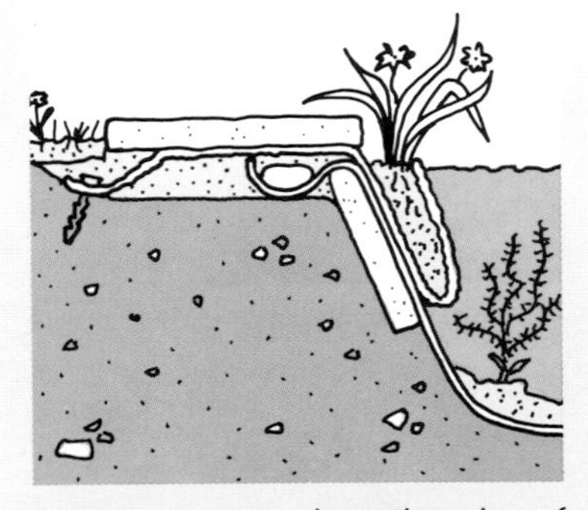

2. Stone squares along the edge of a pool, with plant pockets for planting a steep bank.

3. A way to "catproof" the pool's border is to edge it with stone squares that jut out over the water.

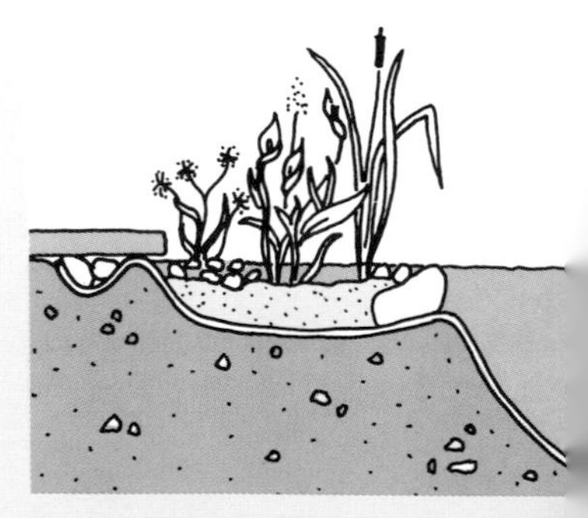

4. A pool border that can be walked on and that has a strip of marsh set off from the pool proper by rocks.

5. Build a loose-rock wall along a steep bank if you want to be able to walk along the water on that side of the pool.

6. Fill spaces between the rocks with earth (do not use mortar), and place a protective pad between the stone wall and the pool liner.

7. Lay the liner and the pad over the wall in such a way that the end of the liner sticks up. Then cover the top of the wall with natural or artificial flagstones.

anchor them in the ground behind the pool liner with special hooks. Flagstones or concrete blocks are placed on top to form a path along the water's edge.

A "Catproof" Pool Edge

Drawing 3

It is easy for cats to catch fish from a steep bank. But a border of square flagstones or concrete blocks jutting out over the water about 8 inches (20 cm) will foil their attempts because fish like kois and goldfish will seek cover underneath the overhanging stones when they sense danger.

The bank can be reinforced with edging stones (see drawing 2) or with a loose-rock wall (see drawings 5–7). To keep the protruding flagstones on top from tipping, they are laid in mortar.

A Walkway Combined with a Marsh Strip

Drawing 4

Along a shallow shore you can simply pull the liner up on the bank, weigh it down with some rocks, and let the end stick up. The rocks will provide enough support for the flagstones on top.

A marshy strip filled with earth should be set off from the pool with rocks that are glued to the liner with silicone adhesive. If the marshy border consists of plants in containers, no rocks are needed to mark the border off from the open water.

Reinforcing the Shore with a Loose-Rock Wall

Drawings 5 to 7

The steeper the bank, the more solid the reinforcement has to be, especially if you want to be able to walk along the pool's edge. A loose-rock wall built of roughly hewn stones or of perforated bricks provides firm support. Build the wall before putting down the pool liner. Dig enough earth away for the wall's width (12–16 inches or 30–40 cm), and then build the wall a layer at a time, filling the spaces between the rocks with earth as you go along. Never build a solid, mortared wall. Place a protective pad between the wall and the pool liner, and pull liner and pad over the wall as shown in drawing 7, making sure that the liner end sticks up. Place the stones for the walkway on top, making sure to add several thick gobs of silicone glue between the stones and the liner.

Wooden Pavement Along the Edge

Drawing 8

If you want to pave the border of your pool, you can use stones or—and this is particularly attractive—disks of wood. Whether your fancy is wood or stone, you will need to lay the pavers in a bed of sand or gravel 4 to 8 inches (10–20 cm) deep. Dig out the entire area to this depth, add the sand or gravel, and then place the stones or wood disks as close together as possible.

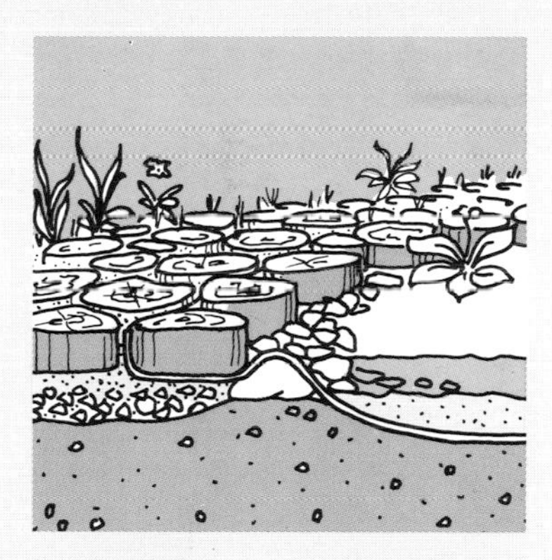

8. Wood disks are laid in a bed of sand just like regular pavers to cover a walking area along the pool's edge.

Along the water's edge you should proceed as follows: First pull the liner over some medium-sized stones, and then place the edge so that the ends stick up between the first and second row of wooden disks. To protect the liner against damage, pour a thin layer of sand on the liner underneath the pavers or use a protective pad.

After you finish laying the pavement, spread around enough sand with a broom to fill in all the cracks between the stones or wood.

Water Fountains and Other Decorative Items for a Garden Pool

Water that is in motion—rippling, cascading, shooting up into the air, or gurgling softly from a bubbler stone—exerts a special fascination for many people. The sight and sound of moving water will make your pool even more irresistible than it already is in itself. If you look at all the devices available under the category of fountains and waterfalls, you may find it hard to keep your imagination from running away with you. You will have to ponder questions like, How much steeper should my waterfall be to approach giving the illusion of a "thundering fall"? Or you will have to decide whether a small pool is large enough for a simple spray fountain; or whether it could accommodate a rotating jet of water; or whether there is room for a multistep waterfall, perhaps with foam or fan spray attachments; or whether a water spout might look better or a gossamer dome fountain that is lit up at night; and so on and on. The list of possibilities is practically endless.

Waterfalls, both large and small, and spray fountains in all their variations are lovely and fun to watch, and anyone who likes them should go ahead and install whatever appeals the most—as long as the chosen items are properly located in the pool.

"Properly located" means that the fountains or falls are set up where they do not disturb the life in the pool. Plants, fish, and other animals do not like to be "rained on" constantly or be in water that moves too much. Thus, if your pool is small and there is no way to set up a separate section for the water fountain (an example of such a separate basin is shown in a drawing on HOW-TO page 47), you may have to do without the fountain. It is best to stick to the following three rules:

- A small pool can accommodate only a small water fountain.
- The more a pool is designed to recreate natural conditions, the quieter the water should be. A "natural" pool should have nothing more dramatic than the gentle splashing of a small waterfall or a bubbler stone at the edge of the pool.
- Fountains that hurl the water up in the air or twirl it around vigorously do not belong in a pool containing fish and should always be installed away from water plants.

A Waterfall

The advantages of a properly constructed waterfall are twofold: On the aesthetic level, the sound of splashing and burbling water invites the beholder to relax and daydream. On the more practical side, a waterfall is useful because oxygen is mixed into the water as it tumbles downward, thus introducing additional oxygen into the pool water. Another argument for considering a waterfall is that there is hardly a pool that cannot be combined with a waterfall. For it is entirely up to you how big the waterfall will be and whether it will enhance or harm the pool.

Here are a few practical tips for setting up a waterfall:

- The necessary drop in height will have to be achieved by artificial means for any waterfall, unless your property is located on the side of a hill. The waterfall will take the shape of a series of steps consisting of flagstones, rock steps, or stream basins.

Previous double page:
A bridge crossing a water-lily pool that has become part of art history. Bridge and pond were designed by Claude Monet for his garden in Giverny near Paris. This scene served as the motif of many paintings chronicling the changes in atmosphere and light in the course of the day.

• The gradient should not be too steep. If the water crashes down with too much force and a deafening noise, this represents a serious disturbance to anything that lives in the pool.
• If a waterfall is of modest size and constructed of relatively light materials (three or four flagstones or square fiberglass basins that look like steps), you can simply pile up enough earth to get the necessary height for the head of the fall and support the steps by burying some large rocks in the soil underneath them.
• If you use heavy stone steps and the waterfall is rather large, more solid reinforcement is required (see HOW-TO page 93).
• The bed of a waterfall is sealed with pool liner unless you use a series of preformed basins.
• Break the flow of the water here and there with stones, so that the water will not move too fast and will churn up more. This helps it get even more saturated with oxygen.

Three small foam bubblers lend a special charm to this flower bed with its stone border.

Water Spouts, Bubbler Stones, and Fountains

Water moving through any of these accessories makes soft splashing noises, and they are suitable for any type of pool. But if they are installed in a pool with plants and animals, they should not be kept running constantly.

A practical way to incorporate any of these devices is to connect them to the water main and run fresh water through them. Of course, you can also run them with water from the pool (with the aid of a pump).

Spray Fountains: These are available in various materials and innumerable shapes—everything from a frog made of ceramic or synthetic material to a seal carved from sandstone.

It is important in installing a spray fountain to protect the liner underneath it with a protective pad and to mount it so that it cannot tip over. Very heavy figures can be mounted on vertically placed posts sunk in a dry wall.

Glue the base of the figure in place with silicone glue. After 24 hours, when the glue has dried, it will not be able to tip.

Bubbler Stones: These can consist of millstones or natural stones with a hole in the middle. Both natural and artificial ones come in different sizes. Complete kits including the bubbler stone, basin, and stones for filling the basin are available.

Splash Fountains: There are two general types of splash fountains. The ones that cause only very minor disturbance in the water are best for the plant and animal life in the pool. These small fountains, which are operated by pumps, should be mounted on a perforated brick with silicone glue.

More powerful fountains that toss water high up into the air can seriously disturb the fish and water lilies in a pool and are therefore best located in a separate basin. That costs more time and money, but in the long run you will find it is the only way you can enjoy both a thriving pool and a very active fountain. Fountain kits complete with basin liner, pump shaft, pump, fountain nozzle, and pump housing are commercially available and easy to install.

If you are determined to have a splash fountain in your pool, then at least install it so that the water will not pour down on the water lilies.

The charm of splashing water. Water that shoots up in the air, breaks up into a shower of sparkling droplets, or drops gurgling down over rocks has always held a special fascination for humans. With a garden pool, if possible connected to a stream, anyone can give free rein to his or her imagination. This is especially true now that some garden centers offer just about everything from simple bubbler stones to water wheels and all kinds of unusual fountains.

Above: A stream-driven water wheel.
Below: A bubbler stone with a bird bath.

Above: Shishi-odoshi, a Japanese bamboo spout.
Below, left: A stone fountain.
Below, right: Spray fountains incorporated into sculptures like this one were once the *sine qua non* of manorial water gardens. Now you can buy them for a reasonable price at garden centers.

Bridges

Bridges, no matter how modest in size, are almost as irresistible to most people as the water itself. Apparently the attraction is not just that a bridge provides a shortcut from one shore to the other but that it allows the observer to get a closer look at the life in the water, to view it from a bird's eye perspective, so to speak.

Whether you have a large or small pool, or whether the stream you want to cross is broad or a mere trickle of water, there is a wide variety of bridges available to choose from. You will find anything from plain wooden foot bridges to more ornamental ones with decorative carvings and on to Italianesque stone bridges in different sizes and widths, both with and without railings. Since these bridges are usually delivered in ready-to-assemble parts, you are not required to have any special skills as a bridge builder. What is important, though, is that the banks on which the ends of the bridge will rest be well reinforced so that there is no danger of the bridge later sinking into the ground or sliding off its footings (see drawings, HOW-TO page 92).

Stepping Stones

Stepping stones can be an attractive alternative to a bridge. Placed a comfortable step's length apart, they allow you to walk around the pool, and they also make fall cleaning chores less cumbersome because they make it so much easier to get at the plants.

Setting up stepping stones is quite simple until you get to a water depth of about 2 feet (60 cm). Two different ways of providing firm footings for stepping stones are shown in the drawings on HOW-TO page 92.

If you want to have stepping stones where the water is deeper, you have to build special concrete piers, which have to be mounted on a solid foundation—a project that is quite expensive and for which you should hire a professional.

A simple solution. The bridge's wooden planks have to rest at both ends on rocks or on wooden posts dug vertically into the ground.

Islands

If you have fantasized about sunbathing, relaxing, and daydreaming on an island equipped with an air mattress and an umbrella, this, too, is a desire that can be realized in a garden pool. If you have a fairly large pool you can pick a spot that is not too deep and—even if you are not an expert builder—fashion such a dream island out of U-shaped concrete blocks and wooden boards and posts available at building supply centers. Instructions can be found on HOW-TO page 93.

These simply constructed islands can also serve as duck islands (see drawing on HOW-TO page 46) or as a marsh bed located in the middle of the pool. If you have in mind such a flowering island, you will need a shallow plastic tub that is set on a U-shaped concrete block with the tub's rim reaching to just below the water's surface. For this purpose, use only those plants that like having permanently "wet feet."

A basic wooden bridge across a stream. You can easily construct one yourself. You need two long supporting timbers to which the boards are nailed or screwed. How to install the bridge is explained on HOW-TO page 92.

Slices of tree trunks serve as stepping stones. Here they are used to form a path across the pond.

HOW-TO: Design Ideas

1. A wooden bridge across a stream or pool requires firm footings at both ends. Make sure it does not rock or sway.

2. A stone bridge requires very solid reinforcement of the bank at both ends to keep it from sinking.

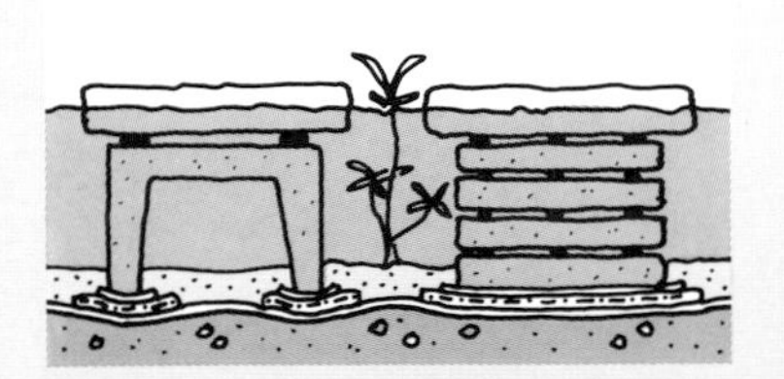

3. In marshy areas and in pools no deeper than 28 inches (70 cm) it is quite easy to build stepping stones, using U-shaped blocks or piers made up of concrete slabs.

How to Further Enhance the Looks of Your Pool

There are various other ways to enhance the looks of a pool apart from the shaping of the border. Some of these ideas are explored in these HOW-TO pages.

Placing a Wooden Bridge

Drawing 1

You can buy wooden bridges in various sizes and models all ready to set up. But in most cases you must prepare the site where the bridge is to stand yourself. To prevent its swaying, rocking, let alone tilting, you have to provide firm footings for it. Here is how to go about it: Dig a hole slightly wider than the width of the bridge. Make it about 16 inches (40 cm) across, and about 20 inches (50 cm) deep. Pour a layer of sand into the bottom and then fill the hole with rocks, leaving just enough room for a square beam that is as long as the bridge is wide. Now pull the liner over the beam and rocks in such a way that the flap points upward. Then place a second beam of equal length on top of the first one and screw them together with lag bolts. To make sure the bridge won't slide sideways, mount angle irons to hold it in place.

Finally, put the bridge in place.

Placing a Stone Bridge

Drawing 2

Very solid footings at both ends are crucial for a stone bridge. U-shaped concrete blocks work well for this purpose. The number of blocks needed will depend on the width of the bridge, because support is required across the entire width of the bridge. On each bank dig a hole big enough to accommodate the necessary number of U-shaped blocks set edge on edge. Place the blocks with the opening of the U pointing away from the water. Raise or lower them to the desired point and align them properly with a level. Now fill in the U-shaped hole with sand or gravel and stretch the liner over the blocks. Again, the liner flaps have to stick up. Cover the liner on top of the U-blocks with a protective pad and place the "corner stone" of the bridge on top of it. Now you are ready to put the bridge in place.

Setting Up Stepping Stones

Drawing 3

Stepping stones in a pool are very practical. They allow you to take care of maintenance chores or have a close look at the animal life in the water without getting your feet wet. You can use a variety of materials to build the piers for the steps: U-shaped concrete blocks, flagstones glued together with silicone adhesive, or perforated bricks. For the actual stepping stones you can use natural or artificial flagstones or roughly hewn rocks. To make sure they will remain solidly in place, attach them to their support with silicone glue. With the help of concrete blocks or flat rocks you can locate the stepping stones in water of various depths up to about 28 inches (70 cm). Steps in higher water are unstable and thus not safe to walk on.

Important: To protect the pool liner against abrasion, be sure to put several pieces of leftover liner and a protective pad underneath the pier supporting the stepping stones.

Constructing a Large Waterfall

Drawing 4

A large waterfall either at the head of a stream (see page 66) or where the stream empties into the pool adds a very special attraction to a garden. But it involves a lot of work because solid reinforcement is needed for the slope. If the water is to tumble over a stretch of 10 feet (3 m) or so, the upper end has to be 28 to 32 inches (70–80 cm) higher than the lower end.

Mark the width, length, and path of the waterfall. The fall doesn't have to descend in a straight line; in fact, a waterfall that forms an S curve or a semicircle looks better. Start working at the highest point. Dig posts of different lengths about halfway into the earth on both sides of the planned falls at fairly large intervals, with the tops of the posts forming a descending line corresponding to the waterfall's gradient. At the head of the falls line up the posts next to each other to form a semicircle, or build a loose-rock or a mortared wall. Connect the other, widely spaced posts with horizontal boards.

Once you have thus created the basic shape of the waterfall, regulate the gradient of the bed by arranging earth, gravel, and wooden beams in steps. Start with a long step at the top, and then let the steps become shorter and shallower and, if possible, wider as well as you approach the inlet. Now position the liner in the stream bed, nailing it to the sides and gluing it to the liner of the pool or stream that the fall empties into (use liner adhesive). Place pebbles and stones on top of the liner to slow the flow of the water.

The water that circulates over the waterfall comes either from the pool or from the collection pit of the stream (see drawing, HOW-TO page 75). A garden hose, attached to a pump, takes the water from the pool or pit to the "spring" at the top.

Building an Island for Sunbathing
Drawing 5
In a large pool there is plenty of room for an island made accessible by a wooden bridge. You can obtain the needed materials at a building supply center or a lumber yard. U-shaped concrete blocks are used to support the island, with a layer of perforated bricks mortared to the top of the blocks (use ready-mix concrete). Lay several pieces of liner and a pad underneath the U-blocks to protect the liner at the bottom of the pool.

The island itself is built of wooden boards that are screwed or nailed to supporting timbers (use rustproof screws or nails). Position the island with the timbers resting on the perforated bricks. A simple wooden bridge is added to provide access to the island. Make sure the shore end of the bridge rests on a firm footing.

4. A large waterfall that either empties into the pool or forms the head of a stream is built with the help of round or square posts and boards. It does not necessarily have to run in a straight line to the pool but can follow an S-curve, have a sharp corner, or form a semicircle.

5. If you want to build an island for sunbathing, you will need a wooden bridge, perforated bricks, U-shaped concrete blocks, and supporting timbers.

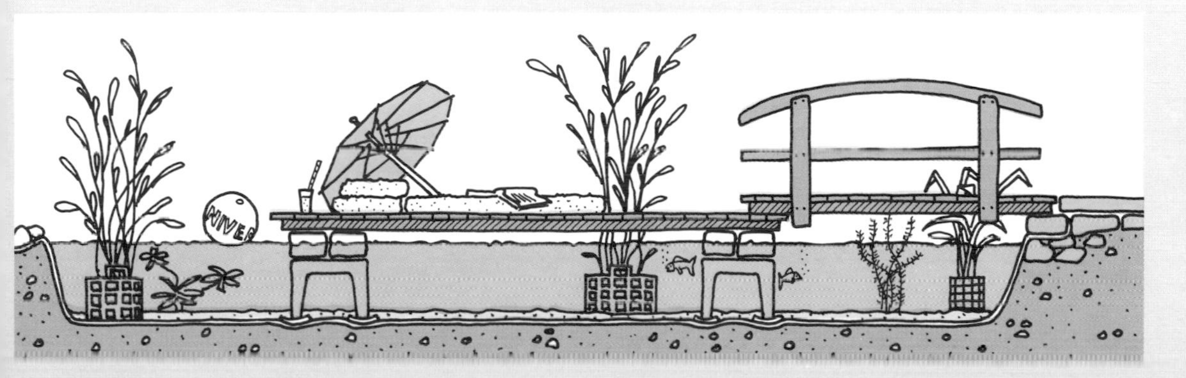

Choosing the Best Green and Flowering Plants

There are many kinds of plants that grow in and near water, and they offer an amazing variety of flowers and colors. For the pool gardener it is important to figure out ahead of time where each plant will do best. Light and warmth are required for good growth, but shade also plays an important role.

Plants account for half the beauty of a pool. Without them, a pool would not only be boring to look at but it also would not function properly, for plants are a crucial link in the chain of life of the pool. As long as a proper balance is maintained between the amount of water and the number of plants and animals, life in the pool will function perfectly. There is no simple formula that tells you how much planting is optimal for a pool, but there is a sufficient body of practical experience and botanical knowledge to help you choose the right plants.

The art of any gardener really consists in knowing plants well enough to place them each in its proper spot. In the case of a "pool gardener," this art is relatively easy to learn if one reflects a little about the way of life of the plants that are to occupy various areas of the pool.

Where to Buy Plants for a Garden Pool

Good places to look for a varied selection of plants suitable for a pool are garden centers, nurseries specializing in aquatic plants, and aquarium supply centers. Or you can select your plants comfortably at home from a catalogue and have them sent by mail. Most mail-order firms have well-illustrated catalogues you can send for, and some of them offer complete plant assortments for pools of different sizes. If you have special desires, these are taken into account in the selection.

Important Reminder: Many pool owners intent on using native plants exclusively think these can be obtained only from the wild. This is far from the truth. Plant experts have been cultivating hardy water and marsh plant varieties for many plant generations, and these strains will adjust without problems to a garden pool and thrive there. Among them are a large number of native plants. You can get anything your heart desires—whether native or exotic—from commercial sources or from other garden pool owners. Don't, therefore, remove any plants from nature. Because wetlands are being eliminated in many areas, occurrence and survival of water and marsh plants are often limited to only a few places. Many endangered species are under protection, and you can get in trouble with the law if you remove plants or their seeds from the wild.

A pool with a dock. The small dock juts out from a narrow terrace bordering the pool. The rhododendron bush, variety "Blue Peter", seems to be especially happy in the permanently humid air of its surroundings.

Practical Tips for Planting

All pool plants are creatures of the water. They can withstand exposure to wind, air, and sun only if they are in constant contact with their true element, water. So if you cannot get around to planting immediately after purchasing plants, make sure they have enough water: Place marsh plants so that their roots stand in water, and immerse any plants with floating leaves (water lilies!) in a container filled with water. For floating plants a shallow pan will do.

Start the project by laying out your planting plan on paper, at least in approximate outline. Otherwise, you may give way to temptation when confronted with the wide choice of available plants and later find that you have bought too many. Depending on the time of year, most garden pool plants look rather sickly when you buy them, but they quickly grow into magnificent specimens that take up a lot of room.

Density of First Planting: The different zones of the pool are planted in different densities. A good rule of thumb is to figure on four to six plants per square yard (1 m^2) in marshy zones and three to four, in shallow-water zones.

• Square yards are too small a unit for determining how many water lilies should be planted. Depending on the vigor of the strain in question, three to five plants are sufficient for a pool of 10 square yards (10 m^2). If you like, you can add some other plant species—floating heart, for instance—that thrives under similar conditions.

• Submerged plants, the most important suppliers of oxygen (see page 101), will grow anywhere in the pool. Figure on about two to three plants per square yard of pool surface. Since most underwater plants proliferate rapidly, you should thin them now and then in the course of the summer.

• Six to eight small plants per square yard will provide plentiful vegetation along the pool's margin in damp or dry soil. If the plants are larger or grow vigorously, two to three will be sufficient.

• When you first plant in and around your pool, follow the motto "less is more." Your pocketbook will be grateful, and you can always add plants at a later date if there are some glaring holes.

Time of Planting: You can plant anytime, from when the ice goes out in the spring to the fall. This is the period of vegetative growth, when plants find everything they need to thrive. You need not worry about plants taking root, even if you plant them in late summer. Since most pool plants are raised in individual pots, there is no danger of root damage when they are transferred to the pool bottom or to your containers, and the plants will quickly take hold in their new location.

Plants that are not fully winter hardy, such as the cardinal flower (*Lobelia cardinalis*), should not be planted until all danger of frost is past.

The half-banded toper *(Sympetrum semicinctum)*, a dazzling skimmer that frequents garden ponds.

Tips for Planting: There is nothing difficult about planting pool plants, but a few rules must be observed:

• Plants that do not root in soil are simply placed loose in the water.

• Plants that root in the bottom, such as the marsh plants and those with floating leaves, can be set directly in the bottom of the pool (if there is soil there) or they can be planted in submerged containers (see drawings, HOW-TO pages 104–105).

• If you use containers, be sure they are large enough. Underwater plants with roots and plants that form runners are placed in large, shallow containers. Containers for larger, and especially for flowering plants, such as flowering rush, lobelia, and the various irises, should be a good 12 inches (30 cm) across.

• The so-called bank planting mats with plant pockets (see drawing, HOW-TO page 82) are especially practical and versatile. Using these mats, one can easily plant even steep banks, separate a marshy area from the regular garden, or hide the plastic or fiberglass edges of pools from view with a carpet of plants.

• Organize the plants in clusters with coordinated colors. Take into account the flowering periods. With a little bit of care, you can choose plants with a view to having something in bloom and adding color to your pool all summer long.

Important: Always place the rhizomes of water lilies horizontally; never plant them vertically into the ground (see drawings, HOW-TO page 105).

Fertilizing: Fertilizing water plants introduces unneeded nutrients into the pool. Pool plants manage perfectly well without being fertilized. Only freshly introduced water lilies benefit from a small dose of a special fertilizer for water plants.

Care of Plants: For most of the summer the pool gardener can relax. All that is needed now and then is to tidy things up a bit or thin plants that are spreading too much. In the fall there are some chores to tend to, depending on the kind of pool you have. These chores are described in the chapter Upkeep and Overwintering (see pages 126–137). You will also find practical advice there on how to keep your pool healthy, how to keep algae from taking over, and what to do if plant pests or diseases turn up.

The Right Soil

Avoiding an excess of nutrients is also a primary concern when choosing plant soil. No matter whether you add soil to the bottom of the pool or whether you set your plants in containers, the soil must always be low in nutrients.

What seems to work well is a mixture of clay and sand in a proportion of 1:3 or 1:4, that is, mixing together one part heavy clay soil and three or four parts sand. You can buy sand at gardening or building supply centers. A grade of up to 1/32 inch (2 mm) is recommended. Most firms will deliver the sand at least as close as your garden gate.

You can add this mixture of clay and sand to the entire bottom of the pool—about 4 inches (10 cm) deep or deeper in places—or use it as soil for plants set in containers. All plants that require neutral soil but don't mind a little lime thrive in this mixture.

Some marsh plants, though, have special soil requirements and need more acidic soil (containing some peat). For them you have to add peat to the soil mixture—generally in the proportion of 1:1:1. Since peat can have an adverse effect on the pool water, it is best to put these acid-loving plants in the marsh bed (see page 38). There, growing in containers, they can be combined with other plants that require more alkaline conditions.

You can also cover the pool bottom with washed sand or gravel.

You are always safe if you use soil that is unfertilized and free of toxic chemicals. Be very careful if you use fertilized soils—don't add fish until 2 or 3 weeks after the plants have been established. Fish do not tolerate any fertilizer at all (poisoning!).

Never use the topsoil (the upper level of the earth you have excavated to create the hole for the pool) or humus from your compost pile in the pool. They are too rich in nutrients.

Papyrus (*Cyperus papyrus*) can grow to between 6 and 10 feet (2–3 m) and needs a protected spot in full sun or partial shade with 4 to 20 inches (10–50 cm) of water. The ancient Egyptians made paper from this plant.

A pool with white water lilies (*Nymphaea alba*) and yellow flag irises (*Iris pseudacorus*). A sight of lavish flower beauty like this fills the heart with joy. The yellow flag, which grows up to 3 feet (1 m) tall, flowers from May to June.

Rana pipiens favors the pool margins. It digs down into the bottom mud for winter or retreats into holes in the bank where frost will not penetrate.

At top: The Siberian iris shown here is a variety called "Sea Gull" It is bred to have white flowers and stay short. Wild Siberian irises are light lilac to dark violet. *Below:* This variety of Japanese iris is called "Embossed". It grows as much as 3 feet (1 m) tall and needs humus-rich, acid soil.

Plants for the Marshy Zone

There are many plants that are excellent for a marshy zone with up to 6 or 8 inches (15–20 cm) of water, which may or may not include wet soil. Not only do these plants display a fascinating variety of blossoms, leaf shapes, and leaf structures, but their way of life is also highly interesting. They are called marsh or wetland plants or, to use a botanical term, helophytes (from the Greek words *helos* = damp lowlands and *phyton* = plant). These are plants that grow with the roots—and in many cases the lowermost shoots as well—submerged in the water.

This description, however, fits only one state of the environmental conditions—probably the ideal one—in which wetland plants are found. For no other environment is as variable as that of wetland plants. Just think of the constant fluctuation of the water table, which can lead to flooding at one time and to temporarily dry conditions at another. Wetland plants have adjusted to these extremes in the course of evolution so that they are able to survive rising and falling water levels, as long as the extreme conditions do not prevail for weeks on end.

Plants with Floating Leaves

Several aquatic plants grow with their roots anchored in the bottom soil and with leaves and flowers that float on the surface of the water, some of them (*Nuphar lutea* and a few *Nymphaea* water lilies) on long stems that even stick out above the water. The floating leaves of some species are so buoyant that they can support the weight of a frog. Plants with floating leaves not only grace a pool with some of the loveliest flowers, but they are also highly beneficial for the pool and the creatures in it because the leaves, mostly very large ones, shade the water, keeping it cooler and richer in oxygen. Water plants with floating leaves can grow in various parts of a pool. Many will thrive anywhere, while others prefer a water depth of 12 to 16 inches (30–40 cm).

The Star of Garden Pools—The Water Lily

Among the plants with floating leaves, water lilies are surely among the most fascinating, colorful, and popular. They are the favorites of many garden pool fanciers. Water lilies are probably the oldest ornamental water plant. Even in the earliest civilizations water lilies were regarded as a symbol of purity and vitality and used to beautify artificial bodies of water.

The Egyptian water lotus (*Nymphaea lotus*), known as "the lotus flower of the Nile," played an important role in religious ceremonies as well as in the daily life of ancient Egypt as early as about 4,000 B.C. Wall paintings, pottery, and many other artifacts attest to this. The water lotus was thought to have magical powers; it was regarded as a symbol of death and was the sacred flower of Osiris.

For the ancient Greeks it was the white water lily that was considered to have magical properties. According to legend, this plant came into being when a nymph died from jealousy, and its flower was used in love potions.

Even the Indians of North and South America ascribe magical powers and ritual importance to water lilies, another sign of the universal appeal these flowers have always exerted and still do.

Survival Artists

Marsh plants are not the only ones that have adapted to changing environmental conditions; some plants with floating leaves also have developed impressive survival strategies. A special kind of adaptation of this sort is exemplified by two plants, water smartweed (*Polygonum amphibium*) and creeping Jenny (*Lysimachia nummularia*). They manage to thrive both on dry land and in the water—as deep as 20 inches (50 cm) or more—where their flowers rise above the water surface. Plants such as these, which develop both a terrestrial and an aquatic form, are called amphibian plants. The surprising thing is that the two forms do not necessarily occur in separate plants. It is quite possible—as is the case with water smartweed—for some shoots to develop into the terrestrial type while other parts of the same plant are aquatic. The terrestrial part is then initially supplied with the necessary moisture by the aquatic part of the plant.

Other pool plants—excepting the wetland types—are not so adept at surviving under environmental conditions that differ from those of their usual habitat.

The special delight of planting around a pool is that it involves the most varied zones. In dry areas, plants like rhododendron benefit from the high air humidity, while plants that belong in the marshy area like to grow in moist soil or even in water. And in the pool itself, some plants drift on the water while others float below the surface or are suspended near the bottom.

Floating Plants

Floating plants are plants that float freely on the water but have well-developed roots. They absorb water, nutrient salts, oxygen, and carbon dioxide mostly through their leaves. They could be regarded as a kind of intermediate type between floating-leaf plants and underwater plants.

In the pool, these plants should be located in the shallow-water zone and in deeper water. They do not do well in the marshy border areas. Duckweed is an exception and will get along with little water "under its feet." Duckweed is useful in many pools because it shades the water, and it is one of the most effective plants at binding nutrients. In duck ponds it is absolutely essential as food for the ducks. Duckweed does have one drawback, though: It grows at a phenomenal rate, and may require careful watching to keep it from getting out of hand.

Underwater Plants—The Pool's Cleaning Crew

Plants that live completely submerged in water use all the surfaces of their roots, leaves, and stems to absorb nutrients and carbon dioxide. They do this all day. At night, they use up oxygen. In most cases the roots serve only to anchor the plants to the bottom, and some species lack roots altogether. Like floating-leaf plants, underwater plants lack rigid tissue and are supported mainly by the water, with some help for staying afloat provided by the air channels in the stems.

Above, left: Sweet flag or calamus (*Acorus calamus*).
Above, right: A sedge (*Carex pseudocyperus*).
Below: Broad-leafed cattails (*Typha latifolia*).

Never expect beautiful flowers or grand decorative effects from underwater plants. But in spite of their lack of ornamental value, these are the most crucial plants in a pool because they combat the two worst threats to a healthy pool life, namely oxygen depletion and oversaturation with nutrients. If these "enemies" take over the pool, dreaded algae follow on their heels. Algae, of course, are as natural to a pool as water fleas and there is no need to worry about them—as long as they don't get out of hand. To keep algae problems from arising, underwater plants are indispensable and our best allies. They perform the all-important task of producing oxygen. Oxygen is used up by animals and microorganisms. These in turn supply the carbon dioxide plants need for the process of photosynthesis. Underwater plants also bind nutrients and thereby take away food from the algae. Therefore, it may be advantageous to introduce plenty of underwater plants into a newly created pool. Just keep an eye on them to make sure the pool does not fill up entirely with vegetation. Moreover, when underwater plants die off, do not let them remain in the pool and thus themselves become a cause of nutrient overload.

Waterweed—An Expert at Self-propagation

Elodea canadensis goes under a number of common names, among them "waterweed," which indicates the plant's prolific nature. The species, a North American native, gained this epithet in Europe, where it first appeared around 1840—having probably clung to boats traveling from Canada to Ireland and Scotland. Europeans first gave it the charming name "water thyme." The plant, however, soon lost its appeal and became known as waterweed: It multiplied at such a phenomenal rate that within 50 years there was not a body of water in Europe that was free of it. But the truly amazing thing is that it spread without producing a single seed. Apparently,

only female plants of this dioecious species emigrated to Europe. (In dioecious plants, each plant has only either male or female reproductive organs.) This meant that no natural production of seeds could take place. Female elodea plants accomplished their amazing conquest by means of nonsexual, vegetative reproduction. Because even tiny fragments can grow into complete plants, waterweed spread like wildfire.

Elodea is nevertheless a welcome and important plant in a pool because it, too, competes for food with algae. If it is kept in bounds during the summer by repeated thinning, and if nine-tenths are removed in the fall, elodea is as efficient at making oxygen available, cleaning the water, and inhibiting algae growth as any other underwater plant. It remains green during the winter and thus continues to supply oxygen even during the cold part of the year.

Bladderwort—An Insect-eating Plant in the Pool

Bladderwort (*Utricularia vulgaris*) is an underwater plant that "swallows" plankton (flagellates and ciliates), water fleas, tiny crustaceans, and other minute organisms into bladderlike sacks growing on its long, floating stems. These useful insect catchers with their pretty, bright yellow flowers that stick up above the water, are especially appreciated for their services if there is an outbreak of water bloom.

Above: Clumps of sedges and fescues combine in a splendid display of grasses bordering a pool.
Below: Hatching dragonflies.

HOW-TO: Planting

1. If you knock the pot gently against a table's edge, the plant is easy to remove, roots and all.

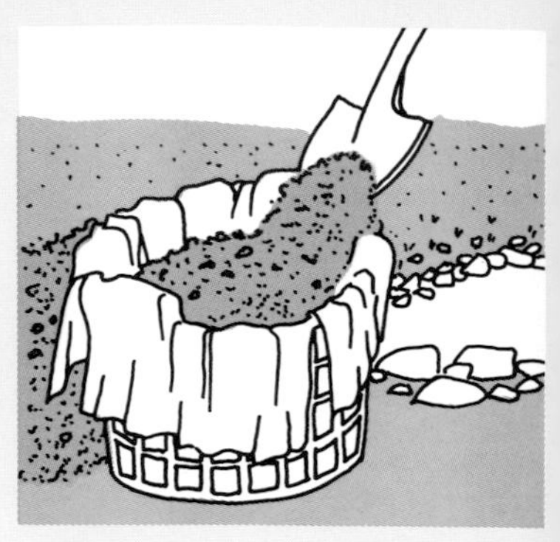

2. Line the container with cloth, and fill it with soil; a mixture of clay and sand is recommended.

3. Make a hollow in the soil and place the plant in it, making sure the roots are not bent upward.

4. Press the earth down gently around the plant, trim off the excess cloth or fold it inward toward the plant, and cover the soil with a thin layer of fine gravel (coarse gravel for koi pools).

Planting in Containers

Setting plants in special plant containers designed for use in garden pools has several advantages. You can do the planting comfortably outside the pool, and you need considerably less bottom soil in the pool or can do without it altogether. Leaving the pool's bottom clear of soil is recommended, especially if the pool will contain burrowing fish that would stir up the soil and muddy the water. Using containers also makes it possible to combine marsh plants with different soil requirements (plants that tolerate lime and those that do not). Simply put each plant in a container with the appropriate type of soil. Additionally, containers prevent plants with a habit of spreading from taking up too much room and crowding out weaker ones.

The Basics of Planting

Water-garden plants are sold loose or in pots. If you buy them in pots, be sure to check that the ball of soil is well laced through with roots but has not turned into a dense, matted mass of roots.

Removing Plants from the Pots

Drawing 1

It is essential that plants sold in solid plastic pots be taken out of them. These pots cannot be used in your pool or garden; if left there, the plants would quickly choke and rot.

To avoid injuring the roots as much as possible, set the pot with the plant in it into a bucket of water until the soil is well soaked (wait until no more air bubbles rise up). Then, if you knock the pot gently against the edge of a table, the ball of soil and roots will come out easily. Loosen the clump carefully with your fingers, and then plant.

Lining the Container and Filling It with Soil

Drawing 2

A good plastic container for water plants is one without solid walls that is more like a basket, with holes to allow the water to pass through. To keep the soil from being washed out, it is therefore necessary to line it with cloth or a thin layer of foam rubber ($^{1}/_{24}$–$^{1}/_{12}$ inch or 1–2 mm thick) that is decayproof. Porous (unglazed) clay pots with wide bottoms are also suitable for use underwater.

A mixture of one part sand to three parts clay makes a good growing medium. Add some crushed charcoal to prevent rotting. Fill two-thirds of the containers with soil. Except in the case of water lilies (see right-hand page), do not add any fertilizer. The plants will flourish fine without it, and fertilizer would only put an unnecessary strain on the water and the fish.

The Actual Planting

Drawing 3

Take a trowel and make a hole in the soil for the plant. If you bought the plants in pots, put the entire clump of soil and roots in the hole. If you have loose plants, trim long roots with a sharp knife to shape the root mass more or less into a ball. When you set the plant in the soil, make sure none of the roots are bent upward. Fill the container with earth to just below the brim, and gently press it down. Be sure the buds of emerging shoots are not covered up.

Watering and Adding a Top Layer of Gravel

Drawing 4

Before you place the container in the pool, the soil in it should be well soaked. The best way to do this is to put the container in a tub and then slowly run some water into the tub so that the soil will become saturated from below.

Next, trim off the excess cloth (or foam rubber) evenly along the rim of the container or bend the ends toward the center.

If you have used a mixture of clay and sand, topping it with gravel is not essential because clay and sand will not rise in the water. But if you have used another planting medium that might float upward you can prevent this by adding a thin layer of gravel on top of the soil.

Planting Water Lilies

Plants whose roots take the form of rhizomes require somewhat different treatment or they may fail to grow properly or even die later. Water lilies, including *Nymphaea alba* and *Nuphar lutea*, are the best known pool plants that have rhizomes, and they are best planted singly in containers.

Preparing the Rhizomes

Drawing 5

Trim the small roots back with a sharp knife and carefully remove any rotten spots. Don't be surprised if the rhizome smells like rotten eggs; that is quite normal. Rhizomes keep growing constantly at the tip and rot in places farther back. The best way to prevent the decaying process is to sprinkle a little activated charcoal on the cuts.

Planting the Rhizomes

Drawing 6

Always place the rhizomes in the soil horizontally, with the eyes or buds for the leaves pointing up. If you stick a rhizome into the ground vertically, the plant will not get established properly. Its growth will be stunted, or it may die.

Adding Soil and Fertilizing

Drawings 7 and 8

A mixture of clay and sand in equal amounts works well for water lilies. However, water lilies—unlike other water plants—need to have a small amount of fertilizer added to the soil. Water lilies bloom better if they get this extra boost at the beginning. But make sure to use only fertilizer meant for aquarium or pool plants, and follow the directions meticulously. Normal fertilizers damage the sensitive skin and respiratory organs of fish.

Fill about two-thirds of the container with soil, place the rhizome horizontally on the soil, and fill all the way. Tamp the soil down gently and water it thoroughly.

Hints for introducing containers with water lilies into the pool:

Water lilies bloom earlier and more profusely if, in the spring, the containers are at first set in shallow water. Wait until the leaves have risen slightly above the water's surface, then move the container into deeper water, so that the leaves are just barely underwater. After a few days the leaf stalks will have stretched enough so that the container can be moved a little deeper once more. Keep doing this until the containers are where you want them to be in the deep-water zone. The chore of moving the containers can be easily accomplished with the help of a boat hook.

If the bank of your pool is such that you cannot simply push the containers into gradually deeper water, pile enough perforated bricks in the desired spot in the pool until the container is at the right "shallow-water" level. As the plants grow, remove one or more bricks as necessary. The only unpleasant aspect of this procedure is that you cannot avoid getting wet, unless you have stepping stones in your pool (see page 90).

5 to 8. Planting water lilies, including *Nymphaea alba and Nuphar lutea*, the right way. All water lilies have rhizomes, which have to be placed in the soil in a horizontal position.

Above, left: Mare's tail (*Hippuris vulgaris*). Its inconspicuous flowers appear from May through August.
Below, left: Water crowfoot (*Ranunculus aquatilis*) provides good shelter for fish fry.
Above, right: Water soldier (*Stratiotes aloides*). This floating plant flowers from June to August.
Below, right: Water smartweed (*Polygonum amphibium*), a plant with floating leaves that needs to be cut back regularly.

Above, left: Bladderwort (*Utricularia vulgaris*). The flowers of this underwater plant reach 6 to 8 inches (15–20 cm) above the water surface. There are many small bladders on the underwater leaves that serve to catch tiny water insects.
Below, left: Water hawthorn or cape pondweed (*Aponogeton distachyos*), a plant for the marginal zone.
Above, right: Pickerelweed (*Pontederia cordata*).
Below, right: Bur reed (*Sparganium emersum*).

HOW-TO: Pool Plants

Plants for Marshy Areas with Moist Soil

These plants require moist soil but do not tolerate permanently wet conditions.

Water forget-me-not — a marsh plant for moist areas.

Bugleweed (*Ajuga reptans*), ◐ – ●, flowers V–VI, blue, pink, white. Ground cover; heavy clay soil with some humus; does not tolerate lime fertilizer; some varieties have beautifully colored leaves.

Cuckoo flower (*Cardamine pratensis*), ☼ – ◐, flowers IV–V, pale lilac. Up to 12" (30 cm), slightly acid soil, easy to propagate; plant in small clusters.

Marsh thistle (*Cirsium palustre*), ☼ – ◐, flowers VII–IX, purple. Up to 5' (1.5 m), biennial, undemanding; prefers slightly acid soil; provides forage for insects.

Thoroughwort (*Eupatorium cannabinum*), ☼ – ◐, flowers VII-IX, dirty pink. Up to 5' (1.5 m), may spread: alkaline soil; provides forage for insects.

Queen-of-the-meadow *(Filipendula ulmaria)*, ☼ – ◐, VI–VIII, yellowish white. Up to 5' (1.5 m), flowers have aromatic scent. Some varieties sold commercially have pink flowers, as does the native American species *F. rubra*.

Water avens (*Geum rivale*), ☼ – ◐, flowers V–VII, brownish purple. Up to 28" (70 cm), undemanding, easy to propagate by division; provides forage for bumblebees.

Japanese iris (*Iris ensata*, formerly *I. kaempferi*), ☼, flowers VI–VII, diverse colors. Up to 28" (70 cm); acid soil; many varieties in all kinds of colors; plant in clusters. Contains skin irritants.

Siberian iris (*Iris sibirica*), ☼ – ◐, flowers V–VI, violet blue. Up to 40" (1 m); forms dense masses. Many varieties (different colors); does not tolerate fertilizers. Contains skin irritants.

Blazing-star (*Liatris spicata*), ☼, flowers VII–X, purple, pink, white. Up to 36" (90 cm), undemanding; neutral soil; plant parts above the soil die off during winter.

Creeping Jenny (*Lysimachia nummularia*), ☼ – ◐, flowers VI–VIII, yellow. Ground cover; grows anywhere from almost dry soil to 6" (15 cm) of water; ideal for banks.

Yellow loosestrife, (*Lysimachia vulgaris*), ☼ – ◐, flowers VI–VIII, golden yellow. Up to 5' (1.5 m), may spread; robust but very sensitive to stagnant water.

Purple loosestrife (*Lythrum salicaria*), ☼, flowers VI–IX, purple. Up to 6' (2 m), hardy; does not mind standing in water; do not combine with spreading plants.

Water forget-me-not (*Myosotis palustris*), ☼ – ◐, flowers V–IX, light blue. Up to 12" (30 cm); everblooming, may spread; slightly acid soil; goes well with marsh marigolds.

Royal fern (*Osmunda regalis*), ☼ – ●, no flowers. Up to 4' (1.2 m); add plenty of peat moss to soil; turns brown in fall.

Butterbur (*Petasites hybridus*), ☼ – ●, flowers III–V, reddish white. Up to 16" (40 cm) during flowering, afterward up to 3' (1 m); spreads and needs regular thinning.

Orchid primrose (*Primula vialii*), ◐ – ●, flowers VI–VIII, scarlet red. Up to 20" (50 cm), everblooming; moist, humus-rich soil; plant in large clusters.

Comfrey (*Symphytum officinale*), ☼ – ●, flowers V–VII, purplish violet, yellowish white. Up to 4' (1.2 m); easy to grow from seed, unproblematic; will flower again if cut back. Contains skin irritants.

Marsh fern (*Thelypteris palustris*), ☼ – ●, no flowers. Up to 32" (80 cm), with bright, light green fronds; acid soil; easy to propagate by division.

Globeflower (*Trollius europaeus*), ☠, ☼ – ●, flowers V–VI, yellow, with delicate scent. Up to 24" (60 cm); slightly acid soil; provides forage for bees and bumblebees.

Plants for Marshy Areas with up to 10 Inches (25 cm) of Water

Such an area should not be lacking near any pool. Not only is this a place for all kinds of plants, but, if planted properly, it also provides a habitat and food for many animals.

Water plaintain — suitable for marshy areas with up to 10" (25 cm) of water.

Sweet flag (*Acorus calamus*), ☼, flowers V–VII, yellowish green, inconspicuous. Up to 4' (1.2 m), undemanding; spreads; propagation only through division. Contains substances irritating to skin and mucous membranes!

Water plantain (*Alisma plantago-aquatica*), ☼ – ◐, flowers VI–VIII, white. Up to 32" (80 cm), uses up nutrients. Spreads; divide root stock after 2 years.

Flowering rush, (*Butomus umbellatus*), ☼, flowers VI–VIII, pinkish white. Up to 4' (1.2 m). Has to stand in water; plant in combination with irises.

Bog arum (*Calla palustris*), ☠, ☼ – ●, flowers V–VII, spathe white, flowers on spadix yellowish. Up to 16" (40 cm); slightly acid soil. The red berries are poisonous!

Marsh marigold (*Caltha palustris*), ☼ – ●, flowers IV–VI, golden yellow. Usually forms cushions 8" (20 cm) thick; roots have to be able to reach into the water; undemanding.

Mare's tail (*Hippuris vulgaris*), ☼, flowers V–VIII, greenish, inconspicuous. Stems up to 6' (2 m); does not tolerate peat, otherwise undemanding.

Water violet (*Hottonia palustris*), ☼, flowers V–VII, white to bluish pink. The 12 to 20 inch long (30–50 cm) stalk rises above the water. Not easy to grow; soft water.

Yellow flag (*Iris pseudacorus*), ☼ – ●, flowers V–VIII, yellow. Up to 32" (80 cm); plant in water in containers; attracts dragonflies. Leaves and stalks contain poisons!

Buckbean (*Menyanthes trifoliata*), ☼ – ◐, flowers V–VI, red. Up to 12" (30 cm); acid soil; otherwise easy to grow.

Water smartweed (*Polygonum amphibium*), ☼ – ◐, flowers VI–IX, pink. Will grow anywhere from moist marsh soil to 20" (50 cm) of water; undemanding; spreads; uses up nutrients. Leaves contain skin irritants!

Yellow water crowfoot (*Ranunculus flabellaris*), ☠, ☼, flowers VI–VIII, golden yellow. Up to 28" (70 cm); evergreen; keeps growing underwater during the winter; undemanding; oxygenator.

Arrowhead (*Sagittaria latifolia*), ☼, flowers VI–VIII, white. Out-of-water leaves grow up to 16" (40 cm) above water surface; undemanding. Competes with algae for nutrients; oxygenator.

Bur reed (*Sparganium*), several species, ☼ – ◐, flowers VI–VIII, greenish. Up to 4' (1.2 m), also grows in deeper water; undemanding; trim roots periodically.

Plants with Floating Leaves

These plants are suitable for water depths of 12 inches (30 cm) or more.

Water lily — a floating-leaf plant suitable for a water depth of more than 12" (30 cm).

Water hawthorn (*Aponogeton distachyos*), ☼, flowers III–X, white. Flowers are vanilla-scented; raise young plants in shallow water; care as for water lilies.

Water starwort (*Callitriche palustris*), ☼ - ●, flowers IV–X, inconspicuous. Water depth up to 24" (60 cm); stays green during winter furnishing oxygen under ice.

Yellow pond lily (*Nuphar lutea*), ☼ - ●, flowers VI–VIII, rich yellow. Water depth up to 6' (2 m); prefers sandy bottom. Dwarf form (*N. pumila*) is better suited for small pools.

White water lily (*Nymphaea alba*), ☼ - ◐, flowers V–VIII, white. Indigenous to Europe, where it is a protected species.

Other water lilies (*Nymphaea* species), ☼ - ◐, flower V–X, many colors. Water depth up to 5' (1.5 m), depending on species. Not all varieties are winter hardy.

Floating heart (*Nymphoides peltata*), ☼ - ◐, flowers VI–VIII, bright yellow. Water depth up to 20" (50 cm); spreads; remove 9/10 of plants in the fall. Provides ideal environment for fish fry.

Water smartweed, (*Polygonum amphibium*), ☼ - ◐, flowers VI–IX, pink. Water depth up to 20" (50 cm); spreads prolifically; thin regularly and remove 9/10 of the plants in fall. Leaves contain skin irritants!

Pondweed (*Potamogeton*), several species, ☼ - ◐, flowers VI–VIII, inconspicuous. Grows anywhere in a pool, furnishes oxygen, cleans the water, and inhibits algae growth; provides refuge for fish fry.

Water crowfoot (*Ranunculus aquatil*), ☠, ☼ - ◐, flowers V–VIII, white. Water depth up to 24" (60 cm), inhibits algae growth; thin regularly and remove leaves in the fall.

Water chestnut (*Trapa natans*), ☼ - ◐, flowers VI–IX, white. Water depth up to 28" (70 cm); uses up nutrients. Mother plant dies in the fall, and fruits overwinter in the pool.

Floating Plants

These plants grow anywhere in a pool.

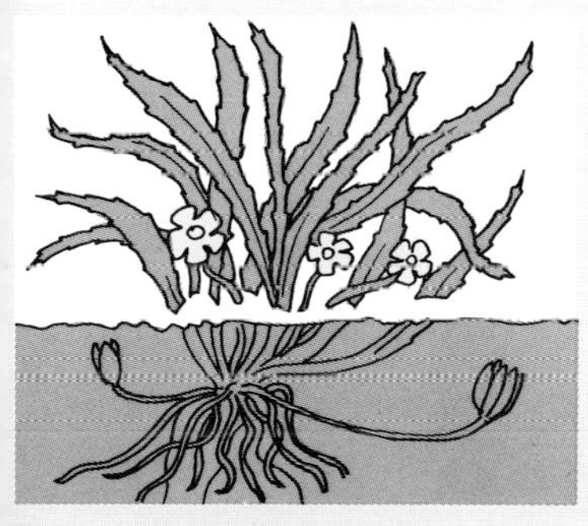

Water soldier — a floating plant.

Fairy moss (*Azolla caroliniana*), ☼ - ◐, no flowers. Inhibits algae. Not winter hardy; fish out of the pool and overwinter a handful in a shallow pan in a light and cool place.

Water hyacinth (*Eichhornia crassipes*), ☼, flowers VIII–IX, pale violet. Flowers only if water temperature is above 68°F (20°C). Can be overwintered only in an aquarium.

Frogbit (*Hydrocharis morsus-ranae*), ☼, flowers VI–VIII, white. Tolerates no lime; easy to propagate by breaking off rosettes.

Duckweed (*Lemna minor*), ☼ - ●, no flowers. Inhibits algae growth; has to be fished out of the pool regularly in the summer; remove 9/10 in the fall.

Water lettuce (*Pistia stratoites*), ☼, no flowers. Inhibits algae growth; water has to be above 59°F (15°C); can be overwintered only in an aquarium.

Floating moss (*Salvinia natans*), ☼ - ◐, no flowers. Inhibits algae growth; should be fished out now and then; loves warmth; reproduces by means of spores.

Water soldier (*Stratiotes aloides*), ☼, flowers VI–VIII, white. Cleanses water, prevents spreading of algae; easy to propagate by separating rosettes.

Submerged Plants

Because of their useful properties—indispensable for maintaining water quality—these plants should not be absent in any garden pool. They supply oxygen and inhibit algae growth because they are heavy feeders and clear the water. Since most of them proliferate rapidly, they have to be thinned regularly in the summer and reduced by 9/10 in the fall to keep the pool from getting choked with vegetation.

Waterweed — an underwater plant.

Hornwort (*Ceratophyllum demersum*), no flowers. Very feathery plant without roots; does not tolerate peat well.

Waterweed (*Elodea canadensis*), flowers V–VIII, white; flowers only rarely. Multiplies entirely by stems growing into new plants.

Water violet (*Hottonia palustris*), flowers V–VII, white to pink. Water depth up to 16" (40 cm); flowers rise up above the water surface. Does not tolerate lime; a sensitive, delicate plant.

Water milfoil (*Myriophyllum spicatum*), flowers VII–IX, pale pink. Inflorescence rises about 6" (15 cm) above the water surface; multiplies through stem pieces or winter buds growing into new plants.

Bladderwort (*Utricularia vulgaris*), flowers VI–VIII, golden yellow. Flowers on stems rise above the water surface; "carnivorous" plant; helps in cases of water bloom.

Grasses, Sedges, Rushes, and Reeds

These plants, which have a special beauty of their own, can be located in various areas in and around a pool. The grasses and grasslike plants described here should be used sparingly and attended to regularly. Almost all of them proliferate rapidly and should therefore be thinned as needed during the summer and quite radically in the spring. Otherwise they may crowd out other plants growing nearby.

Panicled sedge (*Carex paniculata*), ☼ - ◐, for damp banks but no standing water. Up to 3' (1 m), forms hummocks; alkaline soil.

Weeping sedge (*Carex pendula*), ☼ - ●, for damp banks but no stagnant water. 16" to 36" (40–90 cm), winter green, requires non-alkaline soil.

Fake cyperus (*Carex pseudocyperus*), ☼ - ◐, for damp banks but no stagnant water. Up to 3' (1 m); solitary plant; slightly acid soil.

Narrow-leaved cotton grass (*Eriophorum angustifolium*), ☼ - ◐, plant in up to 6" (15 cm) of water. Grows up to 20" (50 cm); acid soil; bears decorative white tufts.

Broad-leaved cotton grass (*Eriophorum latifolium*), ☼ - ◐, plant in up to 6" (15 cm) of water. Grows up to 24" (60 cm); alkaline soil; bears decorative white tufts.

Rushes (*Juncus*), several species, ☼ - ◐, plant in up to 6" (15 cm) of water. Depending on the species, 10" to 32" (25–80 cm) high; slightly acid soil; water cleansing.

Water oat grass (*Lasiagrostis calamagrostis*), ☼, edge of pool, humus-rich soil. Up to 28" (70 cm); flowers profusely VI–X; the clusters of silvery flower heads change color in the fall.

Blue moor-grass (*Molinia caerulea*), ☼ - ◐, edge of pool, humus-rich, damp soil. Up to 20" (50 cm); attractive fall coloring. Aboveground part of hummock dies down in the fall; new shoots develop in late April.

Fountain grass (*Pennisetum compressum*), ☼, edge of pool, humus-rich, damp soil. Up to 28" (70 cm); fluffy, brownish flower heads. Cut back (hand height) in the spring.

Reed (*Phragmites australis*), ☼ - ◐, plant in up to 6" (15 cm) of water. Grows higher than 6' (2 m); important because of its obvious water-cleansing effect; heavy feeder.

Dwarf bamboo (*Sasa pumila*), ☼ - ◐, edge of pool, humus-rich soil. Ground cover.

Bulrush (*Scirpus tabernaemontani*), ☼ - ◐ plant in up to 12" (30 cm) of water. Grows up to 28" (70 cm); undemanding, water cleansing.

Sinarundinaria, ☼ - ◐, edge of pool, damp, humus-rich soil. Winter hardy but should be protected by a layer of dry leaves around plant; can be cut.

Cattail (*Typha*), several species, ☼, plant in up to 20" (25 cm) of water. Depending on species, grows between 1 1/2 -9' (.5–3 m) high; water cleansing; inhibits algae growth. *T. minima* ideal for small pools.

Explanation of symbols

I XII = months of the year when plants flower; ☼ – sun; ◐ – partial shade, ● = shade; ☠ = poisonous plant.

The Japanese pool in the Düsseldorf Nordpark. Japanese gardens, which are based on philosophical principles, are foreign to our Western habits of perception. The idea is for a pool to fit into the surrounding landscape as naturally as possible so that it becomes one with it.

Animals In and Around a Garden Pool

This chapter describes what kinds of animals are likely to turn up in or near a garden pool and what kinds of fish may be introduced. It also gives some examples of how you can artificially create conditions that are conducive to the well-being of animals occurring in the vicinity of your garden, thus offering them an attractive substitute environment. Brief descriptions of the animals' most important habits and behavior patterns will help you get to know wild pool visitors and understand their needs better.

Your garden pool gleams peacefully in the sunlight. A light breeze ruffles its surface, and tiny waves set the water lilies gently rocking. A barely noticeable movement draws your gaze to one of the big, green lily pads. A frog has climbed up on it and now waits, motionless, for some prey to appear. You watch with fascination and simultaneously become aware of many other creature activities in and around the water. There is so much to observe—something new every day. The scenes of animal life you witness around your garden pool will make you forget all the work that went into building the pool and the hours you have to spend on its upkeep.

This chapter introduces you to some of the animals that will move to your garden pool from surrounding nature and tells you what fish you may introduce. It also gives some examples of how you can create a habitat for wild creatures where they will thrive. In addition, short descriptions of the habits and behavior of these pool visitors will help you get to know them better and understand their environmental requirements.

Frogs, Toads, and Other Amphibians

Although amphibians live both in and out of the water, they are dependent on this element for survival. In the absence of water they cannot reproduce. They need water for depositing their eggs, and water is necessary for the larvae to develop until they emerge from it as fully formed frogs, toads or newts. These are fascinating processes, and you will be able to watch them with your own eyes if you are patient and persevering.

Anyone who has spent even a little time studying the life cycle of amphibians will want to turn his or her garden pool into a place that attracts amphibians. Such a nature lover may also want to become active in efforts to protect endangered amphibians and save them from extinction. The fact is that due to the loss of spawning waters the survival of many amphibians—creatures that have lived on Earth for millions of years—is threatened in our industrialized world. Wetlands, bogs, brooks, and ponds are disappearing from the countryside as developments take their place and the landscape is "cleaned up" by draining wet places. Of course, whether or not amphibians in search of new spawning sites will settle in your pool depends to a large extent on where your garden happens to be located. Obviously, densely settled areas and cities are less likely to attract them than regions with fields, woods, and former wetlands or even with other natural garden ponds nearby.

Important: Before exploring what you can do for amphibians in your garden you should be fully aware of what you are not allowed to do: Since many amphibians are protected by environmental law you are not permitted to remove them or their spawn from natural bodies of water. Exceptions used to be permitted, but that is no longer the case under the new environmental protection laws.

Frogs

Depending on the region and the surrounding landscape, the following amphibians may turn up in your pool: Southern leopard frogs (*Rana sphenocephala*), crawfish frogs (*R. areolata*), Northern leopard frogs (*R. pipiens*), pickerel frogs (*R. palustris*), red-legged frogs (*R. aurora*), green frogs (*R. clamitans*), bullfrogs (*R. catesbeiana*).

What You Can Do: You should have a pool that is not too small and has some water lilies. Frogs like to sit on the big water lily pads. There should also be a sunny, shallow bank and a shallow-water area. This area should be filled with plenty of vegetation so that any fish that may be in the pool will not enter it. Reeds provide good hiding places for frogs. For tree frogs, like spring peeper (*Hyla crucifer*) or others, you should also have some dense bushes along the water's edge, preferably willows, whose branches hang down over the water.

Way of Life: Most frogs are both diurnal and nocturnal. This means that if you wish you can see and hear them day and night, especially during breeding season in the spring. Garden pool owners—and especially their neighbors—disagree about the aesthetic merit of frog song, which has on occasion resulted in complaints of "nuisance noise." So far, the courts have ruled in favor of the frogs. If the sound of a frog chorus is not music to your ears or those of your neighbors, try to adopt the attitude of the German animal writer Alfred Brehm. In 1876 he wrote on the subject of frogs that "their voice or singing is as much a part of a spring night as the song of the nightingale. They express boundless joy in simple sounds; indeed, what emerges is a chorus of true unanimity, no matter how unrefined the individual voices may seem to be."

Toads

The most common toad around your pool will probably be the American toad (*Bufo americanus*), the Western toad (*B. boreas*), or Woodhouse's toad (*B. woodhousei*). Others will depend upon the area in which you live.

What You Can Do: Toads may live on dry land, but during mating and spawning season they need shallow water (about 6–14 inches or 15–35 cm) with overhanging tree branches and vines, roots, and aquatic plants. On land these toads prefer original topsoil where they can dig, and they like a pile of rocks built sturdily enough that it will not collapse. Let the rock pile get overgrown with weeds or a ground cover, and do not cut the vegetation back in the summer. This way a damp microclimate can develop with snails and insects the toads can eat.

Way of Life: Once they have spawned, toads may leave the water and live on land. In gardens that retain some wildness and include rock piles and other hiding places, the toads do not usually move too far away from the pool. But if they dislike the surroundings, they may wander as far as 2 miles (3 km) in search of suitable summer and winter quarters. During these journeys they are

A spotted salamander (*Ambystoma maculatum*). This is a rare pool guest. The development of the larvae generally takes place in cool waters in the woods.

Above: Such a quiet pond in the woods, subject only to the changes of the seasons, harbors a great variety of wildlife.
Below: Great blue heron (*Ardea herodias*). These herons like ponds and rivers, both moving water and still. They make their way through the water with slow steps, their long necks extended, as they peer around for fish, their main prey.

exposed to dangers, especially the danger of being run over by cars. If toads do establish themselves in your garden, ask your state fish and wildlife department what you can do to protect the animals. By the way, toads, which used to suffer in the past from a reputation of being disgusting animals and bearers of ill luck, are now regarded with much more appreciation: They prey on slugs, which can be such a pest in the garden.

Important: As a defense against predators, toads secrete toxic fluids from their skin to which some people respond with a strong allergic reaction if it is ingested or otherwise comes in contact with the mucous membranes. If you have handled a toad, be sure to wash your hands promptly and thoroughly. Be careful not to touch your face before you wash your hands. If you should accidentally touch your face and if your eyes become irritated, call your doctor.

Newts

Newts may also turn up at a garden pool. The most common are the Eastern newt (*Notophthalmus viridescens*) and the rough-skinned newt (*Taricha granulosa*). Other newts will depend upon the area in which you live.

What You Can Do: Newts need shallow water with some, but not very dense, vegetation and several hours of sunshine. Make sure no fish live in this area. They also like to have a shady and cool summer home on land where the shady ground is mottled with sunlight. A layer of loose leaf mold and a good cover of plants near the pool (within 6–15 feet or 2–5 m of the water) supply the necessary shade and keep the ground cool. It is important that newts have good hiding places near the water, and either a rock pile as described in connection with toads or a heap of branches and twigs of various sizes interspersed with leaves and compost will serve the purpose. If there are some holes at the bottom of tree trunks or under roots or fallen tree limbs, newts like to move into them.

Way of Life: Newts appear in their spawning waters in early spring. Depending on the species, they stay there a few weeks to a few months and then, in early summer, move into their summer quarters. Most newts overwinter on land in underground cavities where they are safe from freezing; a few spend the winter in the water. While the newts live in the water they are active both day and night; during their terrestrial phase they are entirely nocturnal. Because newts are so well camouflaged, you need a sharp eye and to know what you are looking for if you hope to observe them in the water. They are hard to see on land, too, because they usually stay in their hiding places during the day, waiting until evening before they start hunting for snails and worms.

However, during the mating season (March to April) it is well worth spending some time quietly on the lookout, hoping to witness the courtship display of the newts. The males at this time display bright colors, and both the smooth and the warty newt have impressive combs on the back and tail. The comb and the tail are the most expressive parts of the anatomy during the courtship dance, which sometimes lasts for several hours. The movements of the tail waft a special scent toward the female. If she responds favorably, the male deposits a packet of spermatozoa, which the female immediately picks up in her cloaca. This process is repeated several times. Then the pair separates. The female, using her

Its colors help camouflage this frog (*Rana catesbeiana*) as it sits among in the reeds, waiting to capture some passing insect.

Small animal life in a pond.
Above, left: A water strider.
Middle, left: A frog tadpole.
Below, left: Phantom midge larva.
Right: Freshly hatched tadpoles. There is so much to watch and observe at a pool: for example, the water striders that skim elegantly across the water surface and grab insects with their front legs. You can see the external gills on both sides of the head of tadpoles soon after they hatch. Later on the gills are internalized.

hindlegs, now attaches one egg after another to leaves of water plants (such as waterweed). To hide the eggs, she carefully folds the leaves over. The eggs hatch into elongated larvae with easily visible external gills (respiratory organs). They are agile swimmers and hunt around for water fleas and other live food. In June or July the adults leave the water, as do the juveniles later on. They do not generally return until the following spring.

The Wonderful World of Insects

Insects will be the first animals to "discover" your newly built pool. Within a few weeks you will see things like backswimmers, whirligig beetles, water striders, predaceous diving beetles, and water spiders. In time they will be followed by colorful dragonflies and butterflies. It may be necessary, though, for you to enhance the living conditions for these creatures or, perhaps, even to create them first.

Dragonflies and Damselflies

Around your garden pool you may expect to see green darners (*Anax junius*), *Celithemis elisa, Ischnura verticalis, Enallagma civile*, the blue darner (*Aeshna verticalis*), and other species.

What You Can Do: A pool conceived in imitation of a natural pond, with a loosely planted shallow area where there are no fish, is ideal for these insects. Here they can deposit their eggs, and here the voracious and carnivorous nymphs develop. During the long larval stage, which in some species lasts over two years, other insects

Above, left: Whirligig beetle.
Below, left: Waterscorpion.
Above, middle: Larva of a whirligig beetle.
Below, middle: An immature newt.
Above, right: Phantom midge.
Below, right: Water spider.

and other small creatures provide the necessary food. You should plant some reeds and cattails along the bank so that the nymphs can climb out of the water shortly before they hatch.

Way of Life: Once the incubation period is over, the nymphs crawl up on plant stems to hatch there. From the chitinous shell of the chubby-looking larva now emerges a graceful, iridescent flying insect. Exercising their transparent wings, which sparkle in the sun, the adult dragonflies display their dazzling flying skills. They chase insects at speeds of over 30 mph (50 km/h), but they can also hover motionless in the air like helicopters; they are able to execute loops in the air and even to fly backward. Witnessing the transformation of nymphs into adult dragonflies, watching their artful flight, and getting a glimpse of the "mating wheel" formed when the male grasps the female near the head with the pincerlike claspers at the end of its body are all memorable experiences.

Here are some other interesting facts: The female whirligig beetle lays up to 500 eggs in damp, hidden places on land. After hatching, the larvae crawl into the water, where they grow to a length of 1¼ inches (30 mm), but they return back onto land to pupate. Diving and whirligig beetles catch small water creatures of all kinds by quickly clamping their legs around the victim.

Butterflies

Like many other types of animals, many butterflies are endangered. Their natural habitat is disappearing, and the heavy application of fertilizers and pesticides is destroying the plant species the larvae need to feed on.

What You Can Do: Obviously the best thing to do would be to preserve and restore areas of natural habitat, but you can do some good even in your own backyard. For instance, you can grow the kind of plants butterflies like to feed on, and—this is crucial—refrain from using chemical pesticides. A meadow with wild flowers is ideal.

Polyommatus icarus visiting a flower.

"Pure nature" in the garden. A pool set up in imitation of nature provides a refuge for all kinds of native plants and animals whose natural habitat, the wetlands, has almost disappeared. These flourishing stands of purple loosestrife and water lilies almost make one forget that this pool is the work of humans.

Scythe it only in June and August, early in the morning when it is still wet with dew. If you are unable to do this, grow plants like nettles, thistles, hawthorn, elderberry, grasses, bird's foot trefoil, and violets.

Way of Life: The life history of butterflies is fascinating. The eggs turn into larvae, which grow and shed their skins several times. After the last shedding, the larvae turn into pupae, and at the end of this stage the fully formed butterfly squeezes its way out of its enveloping case. Among the brightly colored butterflies you may occasionally spot an inconspicuous, brownish white moth near your pool, *Nymphula nymphaeata*, whose visits are not so welcome because the voracious larvae of this species can do some damage to water lilies. *N. nymphaeata* is an aquatic moth whose entire larval development—from egg to pupa—takes place in the water. In the spring the eggs are attached to the underside of floating leaves. Later the larvae cut shield-shaped pieces from the edges of the leaves. They build cases out of the leaves and then live in them until the pupal stage. The larvae feed on plants like pondweed and water lilies. Evidence of the larvae's presence is clearly visible in the lily pads. Generally, however, healthy water lilies are not seriously affected by these nibblers. But to keep the damage down to a minimum, you may want to pick off the larva cases by hand or remove the pads that are riddled. Never, under any circumstances, resort to pesticides of any sort. These are poisonous and would have a catastrophic effect on the pool. If fish are present in the pool in proper numbers, *N. nymphaeata* do not usually get out of hand.

A skimmer. Covered with morning dew, this pool visitor looks like a sparkling jewel. It is the only member of its genus with markings on the tips of the wings.

Fish in a Garden Pool

Many garden pool owners are eager to have fish. They may find the opalescent colors of goldfish and koi irresistible, or they may like the idea of having native fish in their pools. The important points to remember if fish are to inhabit a pool have already been covered in the descriptions of pool models (see pages 18–47). What follows here are brief descriptions of those fish that can be kept in garden pools. Some rules and special tips for keeping fish are given to help you care properly for them.

Pond Fishes

The fishes described here are sometimes available at aquarium or pet stores. The European bitterling, which is now naturalized in North America, is a protected species and may not be taken from natural waters in its native habitat. As a general rule you are not permitted to take fish from public or private waters without permission from state or federal officials or from the landowner.

Bitterling (*Rhodeus sericeus sericeus*): This Japanese strain of the Asiatic bitterling is sold by pet stores. It is usually kept in garden pools. The European bitterling (*R. sericeus amarus*) is a protected species and only rarely available from dealers.

Bitterlings, which have an iridescent, bluish green lateral stripe at the base of the tail, live in schools, and you should therefore get no less than four to six. They reproduce only if *Unio* or *Anodonta* mussels are present. Bitterlings need a clearly delineated area with a sandy bottom and a few plants in the shallow-water zone to spawn.

Above: A black damselfly *(Calopteryx maculatum)*.
Below, left: An amberwing skimmer *(Perithemis tenera)*.
Below, right: A green clearwing *(Erythemis simplicicolis)*.

in. The mussels are best kept in a large plant container filled with sand (but no plants).

Brook stickleback (*Evcalia inconstans*): The obvious distinguishing feature of this fish is the spines on the dorsal fin that can be raised. During the spawning season males claim territories that they defend against rivals of their own species and against other fish. Sticklebacks build nests on the bottom. The eggs are guarded by the male, who keeps waving his tail to move water over them and who defends them against enemies (photos on next page). Since sticklebacks are carnivorous and will eat anything that moves and is not too big to be swallowed, no more than two pairs should be introduced into a pool. Acclimation is problematic. That is why it is best to keep them first in an aquarium or in a separate pool. Otherwise the fish may languish and tend to get infested with fungi. Since the

brook stickleback is prolific, it is best to give away the young fish.

Phoxinus phoxinus: These are well suited for small pools. A population of five to seven fish is recommended. If the water quality is poor, the fish tend to develop tumors and fungal diseases. That is why it is important to monitor the nitrite–nitrate concentration regularly. A well functioning filter is essential. Better yet, connect the pool to a stream.

During mating time both males and females develop spawn blisters or vesicles on the body (looking like grains of cream of wheat). Spawn is deposited on stones and plants between April and July. The fry grow very slowly and do not reach sexual maturity until the third or fourth year.

Golden orfes, which are cultivated varieties of *Leuciscus idus.* These fish are very well suited for an ornamental pool. They like to eat mosquitoes and all kinds of water insects.

Gudgeon (*Gobio gobio*): This lively swarm fish is usually grayish green with a silver underside and dark rims on the scales. In small pools with other kinds of fish, introduce two to four fish; for larger ponds a small swarm (five to nine fish) is recommended. These fish rarely reproduce in garden pools. They keep the larvae of predaceous diving beetles from getting too numerous.

Leucaspius delineatus: These pretty fish with their bluish gray backs and silvery sides should be kept in small groups (at least five to nine fish). Depending on the size of the pool they may be quite prolific, laying their eggs in "spawn strings" between plants in shallow water.

Orfe (*Leuciscus idus*): The wild form of this species is seldom kept in garden pools. But there exists a lovely cultivated strain, the "golden orfe," that is golden or orange colored. These fish are highly recommended for garden pools because they eat insects (mosquitoes and other water insects). A small swarm of at least ten fish works out well. Golden orfes need absolutely clean, oxygen-rich water because they are extremely sensitive to oxygen depletion (they gasp for air underneath the water surface).

If the nitrite–nitrate concentration is too high, they quickly develop open sores and tumors and need medication (available from pet or aquarium stores). They do not reproduce in a garden pool.

A stickleback (*Gasterosteus* sp.) building a nest and engaging in parental care.
From left to right: The male, wearing his resplendent courtship colors, is building a tube-shaped nest on the bottom of a pool. As soon as he nudges the female at the base of her tail with his head, she swims into the nest to deposit the eggs. The male then fertilizes them. It is the male who looks after the eggs and young, fanning water over the nest, for instance, or defending it against predators.

Alburnus alburnus: These lively swimmers with their bright, silvery bodies should be kept in small groups (six to eight fish). They need clear, cool, oxygen-rich water with a slight current (water temperature between 57°–64°F or 14°–18°C from March through October). These fish keep the mosquito population down because they feed mostly on larvae of biting mosquitoes. Because they thrive only within such a narrow temperature range they cannot be kept in all pools.

Ornamental Fishes

In the chapter on pool models we have already discussed at some length the special requirements—both of pool construction and upkeep—that have to be met for a pool that will have goldfish or koi in it (see A Goldfish Pool, page 26, and A Koi Pool, page 29). What follows is simply a brief summary of the basic points.

Goldfish and Kois: Both species, including all the different varieties that have been developed, need clean, oxygen-rich water. The necessary aeration can generally be achieved only with the help of a well-functioning filter or a stream of sufficient length. The pool should not be too small. The fish have to be given special goldfish or koi food. Remember that not all goldfish varieties are suitable for spending the entire year in a pool.

Ten Rules for Keeping Fish

1. Buy only healthy fish. Healthy fish have clear eyes; the belly is neither concave nor bloated; the fins are not frayed; the skin is clean and without injuries; no scales are missing; and the fish swim around actively.
2. Introduce only those kinds of fish you know are well adapted to living in a garden pool.
3. Do not start with too many fish (specific numbers are given in the

Kois at feeding time. These fish become amazingly tame, and once they have become used to a feeding place, they will gather there at a signal like the clapping of hands. They can even be taught to take food from the hand.

descriptions of different fish species, pages 120–123) because most of them will multiply in a pool.

4. If you have a new pool, wait about three weeks before introducing fish; by then a relatively stable water quality will have been established.

5. Place in the pool the unopened plastic bag you received the fish in at the aquarium store and let it float on the surface until the water in the bag (usually about 64°F or 18°C) and the pool water are about the same temperature.

6. Do not feed the new fish for the first two days.

7. Once you start regular feeding, give the fish no more food than they will consume quickly. Fish food that drifts to the bottom lowers the water quality.

8. Watch the behavior of your fish regularly. If they start acting strangely, check the water quality and immediately take steps to restore the correct conditions (see page 128).

9. If there are sick fish, there is little point in catching them and trying to treat them in an aquarium. It is always necessary to treat the entire pool. Aquarium supplies dealers sell medications. Describe the signs of illness you have observed in accurate detail; this is the only way the dealer can help you diagnose the problem and recommend treatment. Be sure you follow directions carefully.

10. Leave the fish in the pool over the winter only if there is a deep enough zone (over 32 inches or 80 cm); otherwise overwinter the fish in an aquarium. Stop feeding the fish as soon as the water temperature drops below 54°F (12°C), and do not resume feeding in the spring until the water temperature rises again above 54°F.

Even if you have not introduced any fish into your pool, you may find fish there some day and wonder where they came from. Usually these unexpected pool inhabitants have been imported by water birds, which may have picked up the sticky spawn on their legs or feathers in a nearby pond or other body of water.

Left, top: Southern redbelly dace *(Phoxinus erythrogaster)*.
Left, center: Bluefin killifish *(Lucania goodei)*.
Left, bottom: Golden shiners *(Notemigonus chrysoleucas)*.
Above: Green sunfish *(Lepomis cyanellus)*.

Upkeep and Overwintering

If a pool is built properly and includes a well-balanced variety of plants, the basis for a healthy pool life has been established. However, if you do not want to let Nature simply take her course, the way you would with a natural pond, some maintenance chores are required throughout the year. During the warm season only a few minor things need be done as a rule, such as thinning plants and checking the water quality. But as soon as it turns colder, it is time to think about getting the pool ready for winter, especially if there are fish in it. Some preparations are necessary for the animals and plants to survive the winter in good shape and lend new life to the pool in the spring.

In maintaining a pool, the most important thing to watch is the water quality. Proper planting, periodic checking of the water properties, and adequate preparations for winter will keep the pool in good condition, making it a place where plants and animals will be healthy and happy all year round.

What You Need to Know About Water

For many a pool owner the picture of a perfect pool is one of crystal clear water whose mirror-smooth surface sparkles in the sunlight and reflects the blue sky. But pool water that is transparent down to the bottom is not necessarily healthy water. There are many processes that go on in the water and that sometimes change its appearance, and occasionally cloudy water is not necessarily a sign that something has "gone wrong." You also have to remember that water looks different under an overcast sky than in bright sunlight or after heavy rains. Water is not just a life-giving substance; it is an element that also has a life of its own with measurable properties that can change. Water can be hard or soft, acidic or alkaline, and it can contain chemical substances that may be beneficial or harmful to the organisms in it. You therefore have to pay some attention to the water in your pool, so that the life that exists in it can function smoothly.

The Correct Water for a Pool

Tap water can be used for a garden pool without any special treatment in most areas. In some places, though, it may contain too many nitrates. This can be the case if residues from fertilizers used in agriculture have seeped into the ground water (see Nitrite–Nitrate Concentration, page 128). To be sure, aquatic plants are able to absorb these substances in time, but in the short run excess nitrites and nitrates can give rise to increased algae growth. If the tap water contains too many nitrates, the addition of a water restorative (available from pet or aquarium stores) is recommended.

Rain water can also be used in the pool. If you collect water from your roof, running it in a gutter to a cistern, do not catch the rain after a lengthy dry period until most of the dirt has been washed down off the roof.

Imaginative planning of the pool's margin. The addition of a round wooden terrace, complete with table and a couple of chairs, and of an octogonal pavilion turns this pool into an especially attractive spot.

Filling the Pool and Changing the Water

Always let the water run in very slowly. If you use tap water, attach a spray nozzle to the hose; the fine spray helps dissipate the chlorine. Too much chlorine can cause burning of the gills in fish.

In an ornamental pool with fish you should change about a third of the water every three weeks, if possible. When you change all the water, as in the fall cleanup (see page 130), it is a good idea to add a water restorative.

In a natural pond the water needs to be changed only if there is a significant problem (such as extreme algae growth). If the water surface in a small natural pond has dropped dramatically and no rain is likely for some time, you can add some water very slowly.

Important: In order to get water out of a pool you need a water pump that is attached to a long hose. Be sure to cover the suction opening of the pump with a strainer basket (available at aquarium stores); otherwise it will get clogged with plant material and detritus.

When draining the pool or changing the water you can let the water run out into the garden, assuming that the soil will absorb it rapidly enough. If not, it is better to run it through a hose into a storm drain. Never let the water drain onto a neighbor's property.

In case of water damage it is always the person (property owner or tenant) who installed the water supply and drainage system of a pool who is liable. If, for instance, a leaky pipe or improper drainage causes flooding or washing on a neighbor's property, the person responsible for the problem has to pay for the damage.

Measuring the Water Properties

Whether or not plants and animals thrive in a pool depends on the quality of the water. The crucial factors are the degree of acidity, the nitrite–nitrate concentration, and the hardness of the water. They can all be measured with simple and inexpensive test kits. The results will tell you if a problematic situation exists that requires correction. That is why you should have a basic understanding of the most important water properties. Test kits of various kinds are available at pet and aquarium stores. They make it easy to determine the exact water quality quickly, and they come with precise and easy-to-follow directions.

In ornamental pools periodic water checks and—if called for—quick action are important. In natural ponds with few or no fish these checks are not as crucial but are nevertheless useful from time to time.

The water chestnut *(Trapa natans)* is an aquatic plant with floating leaves. It grows in water up to 28 inches (70 cm) deep. In the fall the plant turns red and dies while the fruits sink to the bottom where they overwinter. It is important not to throw them out inadvertently in the course of the fall cleaning when the mother plants are removed.

The Acidity of Water

The degree of acidity of water is expressed in terms of a pH value. A pH of 7 represents neutral water. Anything below (0 to 6.9) indicates acidic water, and anything above (7.1–14) indicates alkaline water.

The proper pH range at which fish thrive is either 6.5 to 7 (slightly acidic) or 7.1 to 8.5 (slightly alkaline). Water with a pH of less than 6 can endanger the fish.

The pH of a pool can fluctuate somewhat in the course of the year and even in the course of a day as a result of weather and plants. This is normal and does not harm the fish.

You should measure the pH of the pool water from time to time. Heavy downpours, for instance, can affect the pH adversely. Measuring the pH is especially important in the fall when great masses of dry leaves may suddenly blow into the pool. As bacteria break down the leaves, they release humic acid, which quickly lowers the pH value to around 5 and less. This means death for most fish.

The pH must be corrected if it deviates from the levels required by the fish. Immediately change a third of the water. Repeat if necessary.

The Nitrite–Nitrate Concentration

Since a proper nitrite–nitrate concentration is extremely important for the well-being of the fish, you should definitely check it regularly.

You do not have to be a chemist to do the checking (the procedure is simple), but you should have some understanding of what is involved. Chemical processes are continually going on in the water of a pool as bacteria break down organic plant and animal tissue (wilting and dead plant parts, fish excreta, other animals, food remains). In the course of this breakdown activity nitrite (NO_2) is produced, which is poisonous for fish. The nitrite is in turn changed into nitrate (NO_3), which is not harmful to fish. In this process oxygen is withdrawn from the water. As long as plenty of oxygen remains in the water and not too many waste products are present, this cyclical process functions fine. When the nitrite–nitrate concentration remains low enough, it does not interfere with the well-being of the fish.

Too high a nitrite–nitrate level is harmful not only to the fish but to the entire pool. The excess of nutrients stimulates increased algae growth. A high nitrite concentration causes poisoning symptoms in the fish, and the shortage of oxygen drives them to the water surface, where they gasp for air.

Preventive measures are especially important in ornamental pools that contain fish. There you should definitely change a third of the water every three weeks and be careful to feed the fish properly. A very effective way to prevent a nitrite–nitrate imbalance is to set up a stream that will act as a biological filter (see page 67).

An emergency measure, especially if your fish are already gasping for air at the surface, is to change a third of the water immediately and add a water restorative to the pool (follow instructions for use!).

Water Hardness

The amount of mineral matter, such as calcium and magnesium, in the water determines its degree of total hardness. Total hardness is measured in parts per million or degrees of dH (dH stands for *deutsche Härte*, which means German hardness). Usually, water is classified as *soft*, 100 to 150 parts per million (4–8 dH); *medium-hard*, 150 to 300 (8–17 dH); and *hard*, 300 to 535 (17–30 dH).

Most pond fish thrive in medium-hard water, and some also do well in water that is harder than that. Generally, the hardness of tap water is acceptable.

You can find out how hard your tap water is by calling your local water company, or you can measure it yourself with a test kit.

Important for Measuring Water Hardness: It is the carbonate hardness that counts, that is, the amount of calcium and magnesium that is combined with carbonic acid. The carbonate hardness determines to what extent fluctuations in the pH are buffered so that they will not reach extreme levels that would be fatal to many organisms. The carbonate hardness is part of the total hardness and is measured separately from the latter with a chemical test kit.

It is essential that fallen leaves be removed from the water. Otherwise the water quality will deteriorate dangerously.

Pool Maintenance in the Course of the Year

Once a pool is set up and planted properly there are a few minor chores that need to be done in the spring and other more time-consuming ones in the fall. The rest of the time upkeep requires only minimal time.

A Newly Finished Pool

After building and planting your pool, no further work is necessary for a while. You can sit back and enjoy watching things grow. Only the algae, which will appear in any newly created pool, should be examined now and then with a critical eye. If the water is not too rich in nutrients—too high a nutrient level can result, for instance, from using overly fertile plant soil in the pool—the algae will automatically disappear again once enough microorganisms and sprouting plants have become established in the pool. You have to intervene only if green algae, known as water net *(Hydrodictyon)*, are spreading in a thick layer over the water surface. Skim the algae off, preferably with a wooden rake that is not likely to poke holes in the pool liner. Stay away from chemical herbicides—if you don't, your pool will have endless water problems.

Summer—Little Work, All Pleasure

Just about all you have to do during the summer is check to make sure everything is the way it should be. The sooner you notice a change in the quality of the water, the easier it is to correct the situation. Remember also that cleaning up a pool that is choked with vegetation is not only more work than thinning plants as they start to spread but also represents a more drastic change for the entire life community, with sometimes unforeseen consequences.

With any type of pool, except for natural ponds, you should do the following:

- Change and/or replenish the water as needed.
- Check the water quality periodically.
- Thin plants that are spreading too much.
- Feed fish, if there are any, and check their behavior regularly (changes in behavior may signal diseases).

Fall—Getting the Pool Ready for Winter

Not every pool requires a thorough fall cleaning. It all depends on what type of pool you have.

A large natural pond without fish does not need any special preparations for winter. If you wish, you can place a deicer in it.

If the pond begins to fill in, all you need do is remove some of the plants every two or three years and some of the mud that has settled on the bottom. But do not get carried away: What is called for is a minor correction, not a radical cleanup.

Small natural ponds with possibly a few fish in them require a little work in the fall. Change about a third of the water. Remove wilted and dead leaves and trim back plants that grow too vigorously. It is very important to remove all the leaves that have fallen into the water. If there are a lot of trees around, cover the pond with a net. Do not cut back reeds, rushes, and cattails because they keep the water from freezing as quickly, and their hollow stems also aid the exchange of gases. The use of a deicer—preferably with a built-in air pump—is highly recommended.

Ornamental pools that contain fish have to be readied for winter at the latest when the water temperature falls below 54°F (12°C). At this point the metabolism of the fish begins to slow down and they are no longer able to digest food. This metabolic change prepares them for winter.

It is important to take the following steps to avoid problems (like oxygen deficiency or bottom muck) in the spring:

1. Drain off two-thirds of the water.
2. Catch the fish, place them in a large container full of water, and cover it with a cloth.
3. Clean out the pool: Remove detritus, scrub algae off the liner along the pool edges, cut back vigorously growing plants by four-fifths—except for reeds, rushes, cattails, and grasses.

In the picture:
A spring peeper tree frog in some reeds. Adhesive toe discs on both the front and back feet enable it to climb up on trees and bushes.

Water soldier *(Stratoites aloides)*. This plant, which is submerged in the spring and has serrated leaves, does not rise out of the water until it is ready to flower.

4. Transplant water lilies as needed: Cut back flowers, leaves, and shoots (but be careful not to cut off leaf and flower buds); cut rhizomes back by one-third, remove all rotten spots, and replant the rhizomes, if necessary, in a larger container. Winter-hardy kinds are planted in the deepest part of the pool; less hardy ones are overwintered in a cellar where there is no danger of frost. Cover them with dry leaves and check them periodically, cutting away rotten spots that may appear.
5. Fill the pool again with fresh water, adding an appropriate water restorative (available at aquarium stores).
6. Return fish to the pool if there is an adequate deep-water zone; if not, overwinter them in an aquarium.
7. Especially in cold climates small pools with fish in them should be covered (see HOW-TO page 137).
8. It is always important that the pool not freeze over completely. Life continues to go on underneath the ice cover, even though at a slower rate than in warmer weather. You will find instructions on HOW-TO page 136 on how to keep a place open in the ice.

Spring—Getting Set for Summer

In late February or early March it is time to think about the pool again. There is no need for a regular spring cleaning, but there are a few things to attend to.
1. Check the reinforcement of the bank and the edge of the pool; reposition loose rocks or concrete blocks.
2. Clean the drain (see A drainage pit, HOW-TO page 53) if necessary; remove rotting leaves if there are any.
3. Check all the equipment to make sure everything is functioning properly.
4. Start the filter going or the water circling through the stream bed.
5. Place water lilies in the shallow-water zone and, as soon as the leaves start to rise up above the water surface, move them into deeper water, bit by bit, until they are at the proper water depth.
6. Plants that were not cut back in the fall (cattails, reeds, rushes, and grasses) have to be cut back now before they develop new shoots. Be careful not to cut shoots!
7. Test the water and, if necessary, adjust its quality.
8. Do new planting in March.
9. Begin to feed the fish again when the water temperature rises above 54°F (12°C).
10. Do not move fish back from the aquarium into the pool until the water temperature in the pool has risen to within 4 or 5 degrees Fahrenheit (2–3°C) of the water temperature of the aquarium. Release the fish into shallow water!

A Special Tip—Fighting Algae Without Poisons

We should not really speak of "fighting" algae since algae are as much part of a pond or pool as plankton and aquatic plants. A pool without algae is just as unhealthy as one with too much. But keeping algae in their proper bounds is rather difficult, so the word "fight" is rather apt after all.

The reason for excessive algae growth is always an overload of nutrients accompanied by oxygen depletion—a sign that something is out of kilter. As with all troubles, prevention is better than even the best cure. That is why, if you want to avoid algae problems, you should follow all of the succeeding recommendations. Following just one of them will not produce the desired results.

Plants: Make sure you plant your pool properly (see pages 94–109). Plants draw nutrients from the water and thus largely deprive algae of food. Especially submerged plants, such as waterweed and pondweed, clearly inhibit algae growth because they compete for the same food. But floating plants, like duckweed, and plants with floating leaves, like water smartweed, also discourage algae. Since algae grow faster in warmer water, plants that shade the water, such as water lilies, floating heart, and other plants with floating leaves, are good allies because they keep the water temperature down.

Snails: Introduce some snails (for example *Lymnaea stagnalis, Ancylus, Paludina vivipara, Planorbis corneus).* They feed on algae, dead plant parts, animal wastes, and floating debris. Generally, snail populations do not get out of hand; however, in pools with fish you have to watch out that no fish food drifts to the bottom. This extra bonanza would be gobbled up by the snails, which would then reproduce at a greater rate.

The light blue "eyes" of the dwarf forget-me-not *(Myosotis rehsteineri)* look charming along a stream bed. In the fall, all the parts of the plant that are in the water are cut back. Wait until spring to trim the rest, about 2 inches (5 cm) close to the ground.

Building and Maintaining the Pool: In pool construction and maintenance is where you can do the most good, both in the initial stage and later on throughout the year:

- Construct the pool's edge in such a way that even during the heaviest downpours no fertilizer is washed into the pool from the lawn or the garden.
- Check the pH of the pool water periodically. It should be between 6 and 7.5. If necessary, add humic acid (available in extract form at pet or aquarium stores) or hang bags of peat (without added fertilizer!) in the water until the proper condition is reached.
- See to it that the water is aerated enough and there is a sufficient oxygen supply throughout the year. An air pump, as described in page 58, can be kept running all year.
- If you keep fish in your pool, good filtration is of the essence. Either install a special pool filter or set up a stream to function as a biological filter (see page 67).
- Periodically remove visible algae, long strands of algae, and tuft-like formations by hand or with a skimming net.

Improper Measures: Do not use any chemical agents to get rid of algae. These products contain poisons that harm all pool life and get rid of the algae problem only temporarily. After a short time the algae will start growing again, and you are back where you started from.

Following double page:
A streamside scene. In this expertly planned and executed stream the time and effort invested have paid off.

HOW-TO: Overwintering the Pool

Preparations for Proper Overwintering

In the colder regions, the pool and its inhabitants rest in the winter. All life processes and transformation cycles proceed at a much slower rate than in summer. Large pools, and especially natural ponds, can be left as they are for winter. But ornamental pools in which fish and water lilies are to overwinter require some special preparations.

1. A simple deicer of styrofoam uses no electricity and is easy to set up. Put it in the pool in the fall and anchor it down with weights.

2. A deicer equipped with an air pump and an air hose connected to an air stone not only keeps a hole open in the ice but also introduces oxygen into the pool. Very highly recommended for pools where many fish overwinter.

The most important thing: Keep a place open in the ice cover with the help of a deicer, so that oxygen can enter the water and carbon dioxide and methane gases can escape. To prevent oxygen deficiency, it is advisable to keep an air pump with an attached air stone running during the winter. Do not place the air hose of the pump in the deepest spot of the pool. If air escapes there, it will create too much water movement, creating a strain on the fish that would cause them to lose weight. All the devices mentioned here are usually available at garden centers or aquarium stores.

In regions with severe winters, small pools should also be covered to make sure that fish and plants will survive the cold season.

Simple Deicers

Drawing 1

This kind of deicer can be constructed of special, long-lasting styrofoam and a segment of sturdy plastic tubing. It will reliably keep a hole open in the ice down to a temperature of -4°F (-20°C). It uses no electricity but is simply anchored in the deepest part of the pool. It should be combined with an air pump (including air stone).

Deicer with Built-In Air Pump

Drawing 2

This kind of deicer, too, will keep a hole open in the ice, but it requires electricity. Air slits and an air pipe allow for the exchange of oxygen, carbon dioxide, and methane gases. The deicer also contains an air pump, which adds oxygen to the water. The air hose with an attached air stone is placed on the pool bottom at a point of medium depth and weighed down with a rock.

Pool Heater

Drawing 3

This name, which is commonly used, is misleading. The device consists of an electric coil attached to a weather-resistant housing that floats; it does not heat the pool water but, drawing relatively few watts, merely keeps a hole open in the ice. The heater is plugged in during freezing weather; when the temperature rises above freezing, it is unplugged again. The newer models offer an optional attachment ring, designed to keep the hot coil from touching the walls of plastic-lined or fiberglass pools.

If your pool heater should get frozen in, simply turn it on. Never try to chip it out with an ice ax. You'd only frighten the fish and perhaps damage the device, possibly causing a short circuit.

Important: The cable of the pool heater has to be long enough to reach from the pool to the outdoor socket (with ground fault circuit interrupter). Do not use extension cords! And don't use aquarium heaters in a pool!

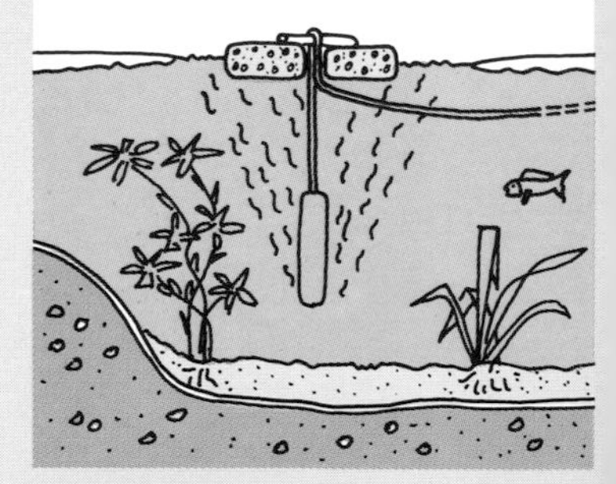

3. A pool heater is turned on when the temperature drops below freezing. It generates only sufficient heat to keep a hole open in the ice.

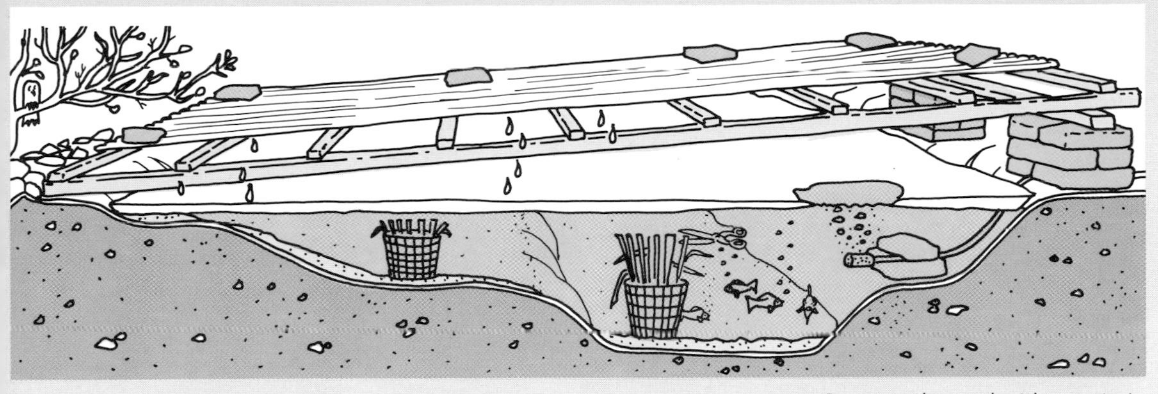

4. Covering the pool with a material that lets light pass through makes sense if fish are to overwinter in the pool. Construct a lath grate for the covering material to rest on. This kind of cover is especially recommended in areas with severe winters.

Covering the Pool

Drawing 4

Small pools of 60 square feet (6 m²) or less with fish and water lilies to be overwintered there should be covered, especially if you live in an area with severe winters and frequent below-freezing temperatures. Pool covers of light, transparent materials use solar heat much the way it is used in a cold frame or greenhouse: The sun heats the air underneath the cover, which slows down the cooling of the water in the fall and delays and lessens ice formation during the winter.

You can cover your pool as soon as you have got it all set for winter (see page 130). The best time to do this is before the trees lose their foliage. This way you prevent leaves from being blown into the pool in great numbers by fall winds, and you save yourself the chore of fishing them out.

Only materials that let the light through are suitable for pool covers. Glass is not recommended because it breaks too easily. Fluted, fiberglass-reinforced plastic is easy to handle and works very well. It keeps its shape and lasts a long time. You can roll it up in the spring and store it for the following winter in the cellar, where it does not take up too much room. It is available at building supply stores.

Before you go out to buy it, measure how long and wide the cover has to be to extend all the way across the pool and overlap the bank securely. The best way is to measure the length and width of the pool and then add half a yard (50 cm) to both dimensions. When setting up the cover, observe the following:

- The cover has to be mounted at a slant, so that the rain on the top and the condensation moisture underneath will run off. The slanted position also ensures weak but essential aeration.
- The slant should face south because the heat of the sun is utilized most efficiently this way.
- Keep an air pump with attached air stone running in the pool to ensure an adequate oxygen supply. Place the air hose in the pool at a medium depth.

When mounting the cover, proceed as follows: Start at the north side of the pool because this is where you have to erect supports for the higher end of the slanting cover. Perforated bricks work best for this; they are cheap and are easy to put away again in the spring. Make several piles—the number depending on the width of the pool—at short distances from each other.

Use laths (1 x 2 inches or 24 x 48 mm) to support the cover. Arrange the laths to form a grate (laths 24–28 inches or 60-80 cm apart).

Now lay the strips of plastic covering over the pool or, more precisely, on top of the laths. It is best to have a strong helper for this; this job is handled much more easily by two people than by one alone.

Finally, weigh down the edges on the long sides—that is, north and south—with rocks so the wind cannot carry the cover off.

Check periodically, particularly on windy days, to make sure the cover is still in place. You should also remove wet, heavy snow. Light powder snow can be left because it provides good additional insulation and helps impede ice formation.

Take the cover off in early spring, as soon as there is no more danger of the pool freezing.

Index

Numbers in **boldface** indicate color photos.

Previous double page:
A rural idyll. This artificial pool brings to mind the village ponds of old.

Photo credits

ngemayer: pp. 122 (above, left nd right), 123; Becker: pp. 2–3, , 9, 10–11, 16–17, 19, 21, 23, 4–25, 34, 37, 38, 40–41, 49, 0, 54–55, 60, 64–65, 76, 77, 9, 80, 81, 84–85, 87, 89 below, right), 91, 95, 98–99, 03 (above), 110–111, 18–119, 127, 129, 134–135, 40–141; Ebert: p. 116 (above, eft), inside back cover (above, ight); Frye: p. 44 (above, left); röger: pp. 4 (above), 13 below), 103 (below); achmann: p. 51; Kahl: pp. 27 below), 29, 124, back cover below, right); Krahmer: p. 120; ayer: pp. 5 (right), 27 (above), 5; Maslowski: pp. 56, 113, 114; Metzger: pp. 68, 106 (above, eft), 116 (left, middle), 131, 44 (above, left and right); forr: pp. 73 (below), 117 above, right), 128; Norman: p. 44 (below, left and right), 5 (above, right and below), 96, 9 (right), 115, 121, 125, 44 (right, middle); Reinhard: p. 26 (above), 28, 70, 106 above, right), 107 (below, left), 16 (right), 122 (below), 144 below, right); Silvestris/Beck: . 144 (below, left); Silvestris/ osing: p. 17 (right); Scherz: p. 59, 102 (below); Schlaback: ront cover, pages 72, 90; Stork: . 89 (above); Strauss: inside ront cover, pp. 1, 4–5 (below), 5, 20, 25 (right), 31, 42, 43, 7, 71, 73 (above), 78, 88, 89 (below, left), 97, 100, 102 (above, left and right), 106 (below, left and right), 107 (above, left and right, and below, right), 132, 133, back cover (above, left and right, below, middle); Tessenow: pp. 13 (above), 14, 69, 114 (above), 116 (below, left), 117 (above, left; below, left; above, middle; below, right); TIPHO: p. 51; TIPHO/Titz: p. 119 (right); Wegler: pp. 32, 33; Welsch: p. 39; Zeininger: p. 26 (below).

The garden pools shown in this book were created by the following: Marry Bauermeister, Cologne (p. 91, below); Richard Bödeker, Mettmann (pp. 64–65, 90, 95, 129); Armin Boyer, Mühlheim (pp. 140–141); Horst Victor Calles, Cologne (p. 87); Degeyter, Bruges (Belgium) (p. 37); Garden Center Hoemann, Langenfeld (p. 76); Brigitte and Walter Normann, Düsseldorf (pp. 10–11); Helgard and Volker Püschel, Mettmann (pp. 19, 50, 72, 79, 127); Horst Schmittges, Mönchengladbach (p. 80, above); Horst Schümmelfeder, Düsseldorf (pp. 54–55); Pieter Schwarze, Krefeld (p. 49); Felix Viell, Düsseldorf (pp. 24–25, 103, above); Henk Weyers, Haarlem (Holland) (front cover, pp. 2–3, 7, 34, 77, 118–119); Konrad Wittich, Pfaffenwiesbach (pp. 23, 80 (below), 81).

Note of Warning

In this book a number of electrical devices and their application in a garden pool are discussed. If you plan to use any of them, remember that only a licensed electrician should handle the installation work. This includes both the installation of outlets for the appliances and the laying of electric cables (see Preventing Accidents, page 56).

To protect your own family as well as others from danger, you should take adequate safety measures (fencing or a grate in the water, see pages 58–59), especially if there are young children in the house or if the pool is located on property with unrestricted access. We highly recommend liability insurance that explicitly covers the pool (see Liability in Case of Accidents, page 61). Every garden pool owner has to make sure that no pool water can possibly run onto a neighbor's property, either above ground or below ground level. That is why it is important to check the water lines regularly for leaks and to change the water or drain the pool properly.

Although almost all of the plants described in this book are available from commercial sources, some of them are considered endangered and may be protected in their natural habitats. Do not collect plants in the wild without first checking federal and state regulations.

The author

Peter Stadelmann is a pet supplies dealer and also works for the Nuremberg Chamber of Commerce and Industry, teaching and administrating tests to prospective dealers in pet supplies. His field of special interest has been for many years the planning, constructing, and planting of garden pools, streams, and water gardens.

Photos on the covers

Front cover: A natural pond with water lilies and wild loosestrife, both yellow and purple. *Back cover:* Above, left: Horsetail; above, right: Frog *(Hyla cinera)*; below, left: Skimmer *(Sympetrum semicintum)*; below, middle: Pickerelweed; below, right: Red-capped Oranda.

Useful books

For further reading on this subject, consult the following books also published by Barron's Educational Series, Inc., Hauppauge, New York:

Kahl, Burkard, *Aquarium Plants*, 1992.
Penzes, Bethen and Tölg, Istvan, *Goldfish and Ornamental Carp*, 1986.
Raethel, Heinz-Sigurd, *The New Duck Handbook*, 1989.
Scheurmann, Ines, *Water Plants in the Aquarium*, 1987.
Vriends, Matthew, *Feeding and Sheltering Backyard Birds*, 1990.
Wilke, Hartmut, *Turtles*, 1991.

The title of the German book is *Gartenteich*.

Translated from the German by Rita and Robert Kimber.

All inquiries should be addressed to:
Barron's Educational Series, Inc.
250 Wireless Boulevard
Hauppauge, NY 11788

Library of Congress Catalog Card No. 91-41774

International Standard Book No. 0-8120-4928-4

Library of Congress Cataloging-in-Publication Data

Stadelmann, Peter.
[Gartenteich. Experten-Rat und praktische Anleitungen. English]
Water gardens : expert advice and practical instructions : ideas for the most beautiful streams, pools, and water gardens / Peter Stadelmann with the collaboration of Renate Weinberger ; color photos by Jurgen Becker, Friedrich Strauss, Aaron Norman, and other nature photographers.
p. cm.
Translation of: Gartenteich. Experten-Rat und praktische Anleitungen.
Includes bibliographical references and index.
ISBN 0-8120-4928-4
1. Water gardens—Handbooks, manuals, etc. I. Weinberger, Renate. II. Title.
SB423.S6713 1992
714—dc20 91 41774
CIP

PRINTED IN HONG KONG
19 18 17 16 15 14 13 12 11 10

Tree frog.

Insects, including many varieties of vividly colored damselflies and dragonflies, will be attracted to a garden pool.

Water strider.

Southern painted turtle.

Black damselfly.

Brook stickleback.

Goldfish—ever popular in garden pools.